I0447839

survive doom

WRAP YOUR HEAD
AROUND
GETTING PREPARED

CHRIS DURYEA

Acknowledgments:

I wish to extend my thanks to the guys at Baum Productions, Rodney Perdew (Moringa Farms), my wife, and the guys of SAR, Tactics, the EOC at both departments for their help, suggestions, and guidance in the preparation of this book, and to my amazing cover artist, who consistently does miracles with my covers. Thank you to you all.

survive doom

Wrap Your Head Around Getting Prepared

CONTENTS

QUICK REFERENCE

Introduction

As a wilderness deputy sheriff, I was called out to recover the body of a young man who was taking pictures of surrounding mountains and valleys, from a roadside pullout. He had been standing at the edge of the road, behind the guard rail. The road and shoulder were icy and slippery. The young man dropped his camera lens cap and it fell just the other side of the guard rail. He stepped over the guard rail to pick up the lens cap and he slipped on the icy rock. He fell about 900' into the canyon at the bottom of the cliff. It was tragic, indeed. His wife witnessed the tragedy, all for a cheap lens cap. The whole accident could have been averted, if the young man had just given thought to the slippery condition of the ground.

This book is about stressing the importance of anticipating the worst case scenario and the tragic consequences possible from careless or thoughtless actions or **inactions**.

Wrap Your Head Around It

If you're looking for the "magic bullet" to survival, there isn't one. We have all become lazy with our modern day conveniences, and while we can imagine a doomsday scenario without them, wouldn't it be nice if someone took us by the hand and led us to the safety of an oasis with the food on the table, our favorite movie on T.V., and the bed already made to crawl in to? I don't pretend, in this booklet, to offer the cure-all for the woes and worries the thought of a pending catastrophe might bring, only ideas, checklists, and shared experiences to (hopefully) get your mind to a place where it can begin to prepare for your survival.

Since mid 2007, the unemployment rate in the United States increased from 6.7% to 9.3%. For those connected directly, or indirectly, to the building industry, it was as though someone had switched the lights off, on or about June 18th of that year. Other industries began to crumble in the months following.

While the Federal Bureau of Labor Statistics reported unemployment leveling off around 9.3%, the truth of the matter is as people began to lose their jobs they began their unemployment insurance claims, and madly searched for new employment. But the economy continued to slide downhill and more and more people lost jobs. With more and more people out of work, the pool of available labor grew proportionately. In the fall of 2009, the BLS reported the recession was showing signs of recovery and they based this claim on the apparent leveling off of new unemployment insurance claims being filed, which is the data base for the BLS reports. Effectively what was taking place was some people found jobs, but at wage levels lower than what they had been paid previously, and the 99 week limit on unemployment benefits began to expire on people who had become unemployed during the initial stages of the recession. The unemployment rate of 9.3% held steady well into 2011, but what it did not reflect was the "turnstile effect" of those dropping off the roles of those receiving unemployment benefits being replaced by new applicants. The real rate of unemployment was increasing, not declining as the BLS reported, because once the unemployed were no longer collecting benefits, they were no longer reported as unemployed. Gallup recently conducted a poll and their statistics reported that the real rate of unemployment is around 21.4% and growing. Not only are more people unemployed now (Spring, 2012) than any time since the Great Depression, but a majority of those who have jobs are underemployed, working part-time, and/or earning a fraction of what they were making pre-2008. I believe (Main Street) Americans are aware of the issues with the economy, the jobs lost, the (criminal) shenanigans of Wall Street and the Federal Reserve Bank (FED), and the burden of debt being loaded onto the back of (declining) American productivity. Meanwhile, the current Administration has added approximately $5.5 Trillion Dollars in debt to the already staggering national debt of $10 Trillion; a 50%+ increase in just 3 years. The $15.6 Trillion debt we now bear exceeds the entire Gross Domestic Product (GDP) of the United States and it will grow considerably higher within a few short years, if our government does not drastically reduce spending. Even as it is today, the only way to sustain this debt is for the FED to continue to print more money, resulting in dilution of the value of the Dollar.

My purpose in writing this booklet is not to be a discourse on economics, but to help you get your head wrapped around the need to begin to think about preparing, what thought processes are critical, and what you might need to survive.

I want to illustrate how economics will play into the many catastrophic disasters looming. Simply put, an economic collapse that will be devastating to our western way of life AND it can arise out of economic collapse itself, or economic collapse can be ignited by a long list of potential catastrophes, the number and likes of which we have never seen before.

You already probably know myriad disasters loom. The geopolitical and economic condition(s) that exist today, hold the potential for chaos. Looming on the horizon are natural disasters and manmade disasters alike. Earthquakes and volcanic eruptions are on the rise, and recent storms have devastated some locales. If you are reading this, you are either in survival mode, will be, believe you could be, or after reading this, will believe you should be. I hope so.

Survival will be an issue. It is not a matter of if, but a matter of when. While I will present a brief assertion as to what I believe the coming catastrophe will be in the following pages, the focus of this booklet is more on what you'll need, what mindset you should have, and how it plays into your survival.

This brief book is intended to provide you with information that can be useful in the event you need to prepare to survive and/or escape a situation that imperils your safety, or in the event you need to provide for your own self-sufficiency. There are many comprehensive survival manuals available. Many are very good sources of survival information and some are nothing more than an editorial from an armchair pundit who has little or no practical experience. I hope you can pick a tidbit or two of helpful information out of this book which is based upon my personal experiences; the exception, of course, is the calamitous catastrophe itself.

This book is <u>not</u> intended to be comprehensive, but rather offer advice, suggestions, and some quick references (checklists) and guidelines to knowledge I have acquired over the years, as well as reference to established and not-so-established practical solutions to help you while in survival mode.

Escaping peril, whether a natural disaster, a hostile and armed action, or an economic collapse, may be the difference between your survival and your demise. Preparation for a catastrophic event is something you should take seriously and do now. Whether you have prepared to ride out the catastrophe at home, a ranch, an outpost, or planned an escape or evacuation (popularly called "bugging out" or "getting out of Dodge"), all require forethought, planning, assembling, learning, and practice, and necessarily within the context of establishing a community or tribe for success.

My experience in survival arises out of over 35 years as a wilderness off road enthusiast, open ocean sailor, and "Open Space" (wilderness) mounted deputy sheriff and training officer in Colorado and California, training other professional first responders in survival and search and rescue techniques. I have hiked the entirety of the John Muir Trail not less than 5 times, spending months at a time in the wilderness.

My expertise in economics comes from a lifetime of study, and having been an NASD Licensed broker and investment adviser for years.

Preparation for survival at a stationary base (home, outpost, or ranch) is essentially the same in theory as planning a bug out; you are preparing to survive adverse conditions, on your own, without the conveniences we take for granted. The events precipitating your decision to stay at a permanent base or to bug out, the details of your preparation, and the degree to which you prepare, and for what length of time you prepare, may all differ, however.

Bugging out to safety may require quick action on your part. Bugging out should be more than just throwing a bag full of camping gear into your car and heading for the hills. Being properly prepared, before you have to bug out, may be the difference between your success and your failure. Being properly prepared, for either riding out the chaos at home, or escaping to safety requires a great deal of forethought and anticipation of any possible threat scenarios; it is getting prepared to respond to the threat scenarios, and practicing your responses. In other words, building your PLAN.

Bugging out may be necessary and it may not. Just because you have assembled a Bug Out Bag (B.O.B.), or grab and go survival gear bag, does not mean you must bug out. The B.O.B. is a life raft, and it's just as usable at home as it is in the woods or desert. The disaster and its potential aftermath will determine whether or not you hit the road. A natural disaster like Hurricane Katrina would have indicated bugging out. A major earthquake might not. An electro-magnetic pulse (EMP) caused by a solar mass ejection or a high altitude nuclear detonation resulting in a power grid shut down might indicate bugging out, and it might not. Impending hostile and armed violence in an area could indicate bugging out, but could prevent it, as well. An economic collapse that resulted in hyperinflation, emptying of shelves, and closure of banks, food and commodity distribution channels, and stores could be caused by any of the above catastrophes, or it could BE the cause, and could indicate a need to bug out. Any of these disasters, manmade or natural, could result in public chaos, as those who did not prepare WILL go in search of essentials (to steal) from those who did prepare.

I won't say much here (but I'll add a bit more later) about a power grid shutdown, except that it is a very real possibility, it could last for months or years, and it would literally throw us back to the lifestyle lived 150 years ago (or more, in that we as a society have forgotten how to live without electricity and its conveniences). A power grid shutdown would be the epitome of the most calamitous catastrophe that could befall us. An economic collapse would accompany an

EMP because our reliance on electronic financial transactions would be wiped out.

Getting Prepared For What?

Mental distress and panic have been responsible for as many deaths as danger itself. I cannot stress emphatically enough how critical it is to remain level headed and calm in dangerous or survival situations. Common sense, anticipation of possible perils ahead of you (in reality and metaphorically speaking), planning, knowledge of your capabilities, strengths, and weaknesses, both physically and mentally, the capabilities of your gear, your level of creativity and ability to improvise, and practice are the essentials that will spell survival or disaster.

You can have all the high tech gear in the world, and all the supplies necessary for extended periods of time while in survival mode on your own, but if you are not physically capable, haven't practiced how to use the gear, or how to deal with stressful situations, your survival is not as assured as if you had. As a law enforcement officer, it was drilled into me, time after time, how important it was to practice different confrontational and situational scenarios, practice keeping cool, and practice with the equipment I had, until doing it and using it became second nature. The saying, "Practice makes perfect", may not be entirely true, but it makes you far better prepared to survive than if you had not practiced at all. I cannot begin to remember all the times throughout my career when my practice had led to a successful outcome of a potentially tragic situation. There were many times I went on a search and rescue callout where the outcome was a tragedy. With just a little forethought, a little improvisation, a little preparation, and void of panic, victims I found, could have easily survived situations that ended fatally.

When you begin to assemble your survival supplies, make sure you learn how to use them. Once you know how to use them well, practice with them in as many mock situations as you can. I will say it again, but I will mention it here as well. Many, maybe most, of your survival supplies you already have in your home, your apartment, or your garage.

The Federal Emergency Management Agency (FEMA), for years, has urged the American public to be prepared for natural disasters, from heavy snow storms and hurricanes to tornados and earthquakes. Most people ignore the message. Nevertheless, FEMA's message has been to prepare to survive on your own for 72 hours.

Excepting persons with medical conditions requiring special medications or medical devices reliant upon conventional facilities and electricity, anyone can survive for 72 hours, as long as rudimentary precautions are taken. The three basic requirements for sustaining life are water, food, and shelter. Provided one is in a physical condition not requiring acute medical care, all one really needs to survive for 72 hours is adequate water and adequate shelter, and any self-administered medications (if critical to the individual). While the human body needs a <u>minimum</u> of 1 liter of water per day, surviving adversities, to include ample water for cooking and personal hygiene, will require 1 gallon per person per day, The term water simply means fresh (sweet) and potable. Shelter, however can mean anything from shelter from climatic elements (heat and cold), to clothing, to shelter from other harm. 72 hours is really not that long, if one provides himself/herself with these provisions, and does not sustain injury or require special medical provisions. Were you to have extra supplies (beyond water and shelter) to survive a 72 hour period, they would be to lend a more amenable comfort level to the situation; but probably not critically necessary.

The whole concept of survival can be put into a nutshell; get out of the way of (avoid), or protect yourself from the harm confronting you. Any other precautions you take, during the first 72 hours, are academic. The emphasis on FEMA's recommendations to be prepared for at least 72 hours should be heeded. FEMA, however, is an incompetent agency and will have little to offer us when the catastrophe hits.

While we might know the duration of the event causing the initial danger (as in tornado or hurricane), we don't know the consequential duration and extent of damage to our conventional infrastructure. This of course, will depend upon the type and severity of the initial event. The victims of Hurricane Katrina, who did not escape the area, suffered immediate consequences, and the disastrous consequences in the aftermath continued to be critical and impacted people of the area for months (and they continue to feel repercussions of the event to this day). My contention is, we usually never know the duration of the consequences of the event, and therefore, preparing for a duration of only 72 hours is somewhat simplistic and could result in not surviving.

Whether the best course of action is getting out of the way of harm, or protecting yourself from it, will be determined by the nature of the danger, and/or your preparedness to confront it. The term "normalcy bias" has become popular to describe a mindset that accepts the status quo as something never threatened. In other words, because something has never happened in our experience, we believe it won't ever happen. History is wrought with examples where people couldn't believe something could happen; to the extent that even the concept eluded them. The normalcy bias lulled them into complacency, and it remains, effectively, a snare waiting for you to walk into. Events that we have not experienced, are not within our frame of reference and thus, if we have not imagined them possible, we cannot have prepared for them. Another danger, somewhat related to the normalcy bias, is "perceived self-exclusion", or "I know it can happen, but it probably won't happen to me.", but that's what the guy to whom it did happen, thought too.

One part of preparation is imagining... anticipating worst case scenarios. I use the plural, scenarios, because we don't know what catastrophe is coming, but there is a long list of very real possibilities.

Anticipating the consequences of our actions, reactions, or actions perpetrated against us is crucial. As a mounted deputy sheriff, I was called out on a search and rescue mission in the San Bernardino Mountains (specifically a vast wilderness area in the San Bernardino National Forest) to search for a lost Boy Scout who had been on a camping trip with his Scout Pack. We had learned the Pack consisted of 15 or so Boy Scouts and two Scout Leaders who were on a three day hiking trip, with two overnight stays at campsites spaced about 10 miles from one another. During the second day out and on the way to the second campsite, one of the Scouts became too exhausted to keep up with the rest of the Pack. The Scout Leaders agreed the campsite was only about 1/2 mile ahead, and decided the rest of the Pack should continue hiking to the campsite and begin to make camp, as the afternoon was closing in on dusk. Figuring the distance was short, the Scout Leaders agreed the one Scout could sit and rest, while they (both of them) continued with the Pack to the campsite, at which time one Leader was to immediately return for the resting Scout. The Scout Leaders had misjudged the actual distance to the campsite, which turned out to be about 2 miles; not a half mile. After reaching the campsite, one Leader immediately returned to get the resting Scout, but by that time the Sun was setting quickly. By the time the Leader reached the spot where they had left the Scout, it was almost completely dark. The Boy Scout was nowhere to be found. What happened? The

Scout Leader wasn't prepared. He did not know the actual distance to the campsite; he had reasoned a 1 mile round trip that turned into a 4 mile round trip. If he had realized the roundtrip would be 4 miles, he should have known that the time it would take him to get to the campsite and return would be well over an hour and it would be dark. He did not anticipate the physical condition, beforehand, of the Scout he left behind, he did not consider the true "wild" nature of the area, and he did not know his terrain. This ended in a tragedy, as the Boy Scout was never found. It could have been avoided if the Scout Leaders had anticipated worst case scenarios. We should be equally anticipatory of the consequences of not preparing for a possible catastrophe that will most certainly confront us.

While there are many, many potential catastrophes, I have listed a few, although not in any specific order of importance or likelihood:

Asteroid Impact (unlikely, but possible)
      Massive continental destruction; nuclear winter for years

Earthquake on the Cascadian Fault of 9.0+
     magnitude (overdue)
     Total destruction along Pacific
     Northwest; Tsunami of 50 feet+
     height throughout northern
     rim Pacific Ocean

Earthquake on the San Andreas Fault of
     7.3+ magnitude (overdue)
     Widespread devastation to California
     cities

Earthquake on the New Madrid Fault of
     8.0+ (overdue)
     Complete devastation for 100 miles
     either side of the Mississippi Valley,
     from the Gulf of Mexico to the Great
     Lakes.

Eruption of the Yellowstone Caldera
     (overdue)
     Complete destruction of Montana,
     Wyoming, Idaho, Northern Nevada,
     and all mid western states. Nuclear
     winter surrounding the globe for
     years

Shift of Geo-Magnetic Poles

Consequences could range from none or little to massive tectonic shifting of continental plates resulting in earthquakes and flooding

Climatic Change (Storms, Drought, etc.)

Extensive impact on food production, including livestock, grains, and other food crops

Nuclear EMP (high altitude detonation) from any hostile entity. Complete power grid failure (civilization thrown back into dark ages for years)

Solar Coronal Mass Ejection (CME). Similar to an EMP. Complete power grid failure (civilization thrown back into dark ages for years)

Nuclear Bomb attack from any hostile entity. Devastation extensive, but otherwise unknown

Massive Terrorist Act (conventional, nuclear, biologic, chemical, dirty bomb, or active shootings) Regional to nationally widespread devastation; emergency responses strained

Cyber Attack (terrorist or other source)
Highly possible, and depending upon severity, could result in temporary disruption to complete power grid failure and "dark ages for years"

Foreign Act of War (very possible)
Middle East conflict turns nuclear and into WWIII (everyday, this is gaining likelihood)

Economic Collapse and Melt-Down (most likely). Devastation described below

And, the list goes on. Some possibilities include Super Storms, Floods, Hurricanes, Tornadoes, Biological or Viral Pandemics, etc. Some are inconceivable; some not so likely and some likely. But, never have there been so many possible catastrophes presenting themselves all at one moment in time, and each one could result in near chaos, or complete chaos. Any of them could result in the failure of our infrastructure, stoppage of food, fuel, and other essential goods and services distribution, failure of local, state, and federal government services, and imposition of curfews and martial law. With the number of catastrophic events that could occur at anytime, <u>the likelihood that one of them (however not specifically which one) might occur, goes up exponentially.</u>

The absolute given and critical concern is that one catastrophic event will involve other reverberating events that result from the initial event. A coronal mass ejection or a series of high altitude nuclear explosions will result in an electromagnetic pulse that will cause a massive shut down of the power grids. A shut down of the power grids will result in extensive disruption of supply chain logistics, resulting in scarcity or outright non-availability of everything from food, fuel, pharmaceuticals, water, gas, and other essentials. Hyperinflation will result as scarcity mounts, as any goods or services remaining available will become exceedingly expensive. An H5N1 flu epidemic, a polar axis shift, a massive earthquake, or an all out thermonuclear war, or any other major catastrophe will all follow with like-calamitous reverberations. It has been said before, I have said it, and it will be said again, while no one can paste a time or date on when catastrophe will strike, it is an absolute given that one, followed by others will strike, and the likelihood of coming catastrophes is mounting faster than any time in memorable history. Those who prepare will more likely survive than those who do not.

It is very well documented, our own government is preparing camps. Whether they are detention camps, refugee camps, or emergency relief centers is not clear, but they are being built as I write this. The government has ordered millions of body bags, it has ordered so many MRE's that purchase orders from commercial vendors to the manufacturers have been pre-empted and are backordered as much as 6 months. The government has ordered 500 million rounds of .40 caliber ammunition, and 200 million rounds of .223 ammunition. Full ballistic and tactical uniform gear has been ordered for government agencies whose role has never been conflict or combat, and the government has ordered thousands of bulletproof, ballistic secure checkpoint booths. One must ask why. What is the preparation for? What do they know that we don't? Where there is smoke, there is usually fire; and smoke is beginning to bellow from unlikely places.

I have heard parables about the Bible story of Noah building his ark. People all over laughed at him, telling him he was crazy. They mocked him as he finished construction of the ark and began to collect wildlife. When the flood waters began to rise, and Noah had sealed his ship, those who had laughed and mocked his preparations, began to beat on the hull and beg to be let aboard.

I did not intend to make this book a "how to book", but I find it difficult to not to address (in a cursory fashion) what you should be doing, and what you will need and need to do for immediate and short term survival, and if the catastrophic reverberations go long term, what you will need to survive for longer periods. In the following chapters I will touch on these subjects, but time is running out and it is time to "WRAP YOUR HEAD AROUND GETTING PREPARED".

Economic Melt-Down

Here is my segue on the economics I discussed in the first paragraphs, and why this is an issue. While none of these (listed) potential catastrophic events can be ruled out, I believe the event that poses the most danger to our way of life is not a solar flare, enemy attack by nuclear weapons, terrorism, acts of God, or cyber attack, although they could be significant contributors, as would an EMP, and most assuredly, all out war would elicit economic collapse. It is the failure of global economies, including our own (which could be advanced by, or involve other catastrophic incidents as well) that I believe is most threatening.

As I write this, the Euro is teetering on the threshold of failure. While no one can be certain if the Euro will be allowed to fail or if it will be saved, debt mounts in European countries where the cost of socialistic programs or maintenance of government expenses exceed the Gross Domestic Product (GDP) of those countries. As the failure of the Euro looms and foreign entities continue to divest themselves of the Euro, placing their investments in the last remaining currencies showing signs of stability, the Dollar will sustain value but only so long as there is an inflow of foreign investment to it via U.S. Treasury purchases by those foreign entities. China holds about $1.5 Trillion in U.S. Notes, Bills, and Bonds; it is the largest single foreign creditor to the U.S. China has already indicated it won't buy anymore U.S. Treasuries, and is trying to divest itself of investment in U.S. debt. So as to not cause further devaluation of the Dollar, as this would mean huge losses for China, it is doing so quietly and discreetly. China is the world's largest producer of gold. By Chinese law, no gold is permitted to leave the country. China is also purchasing large quantities of gold on the open market, with Dollars (currency) produced through the measured sale (on the open market) of their U.S. Treasury holdings. I believe China's move to amass large quantities of gold is a clear indication it is trying to hedge its potential losses as the Dollar declines in value.

Once all Chinese holdings of U.S. debt are divested, all other currency has been exchanged, they have hedged the $1.5 Trillion of debt with gold reserves, and with the Euro either having already failed or on the threshold, investment in the Dollar will decline dramatically. At that time, for the U.S. to continue to pay interest on its $15.6 Trillion debt, it must continue to print money. The more the FED prints money, the more diluted its value becomes, and thus within a few short months the Dollar will face the same collapse the Euro faces today. As the Dollar's value is diluted, it purchases less and thus inflation begins with increasing prices of commodities. Instead of $100 buying a barrel of oil, a barrel of oil will cost $150, then $200, and then $300, or more. The price of gasoline and diesel will rise from over $4.50 per gallon in the U.S. to $10.00 per gallon or higher. A doubling or tripling of the price of oil, that fuels over 40% of our electric power plants, will result in soaring electricity costs or rationing of power. With the increasing price of fuel, transportation costs rise and the cost of production of food stocks and transportation from the farm to the table will increase exponentially. With limiting production, transportation, and rising prices, commodities and goods we take for granted, will become more and more prohibitively expensive and eventually scarce.

The Dollar is currently the world reserve currency. Most international purchases, including oil, take place with the exchange of the Dollar. In addition to hedging its losses due to the declining value of the Dollar and U.S. Treasuries, China's amassing of huge gold reserves, I believe, indicates a move to establish its currency, the Yuan, as the new world reserve currency. As the U.S. debt cannot be sustained by any means other than the FED's printing of money, the Dollar WILL continue to devalue. By losing its status as the world reserve currency, the Dollar will have to be exchanged for the Yuan (or other currency) to enact global financial transactions, including the purchase of oil, food, and other commodities. This alone will drive prices even higher, by manifesting itself in higher prices for all imported goods.

While the subject of this booklet is not about financial preparation, some speculations on protecting your assets are noteworthy. In preparation for an economic collapse, invest as heavily in silver (first), and gold (second) as you can. Hard assets in small denomination, pre-1965 silver coins are best.

Why do I say pre-1965 silver coins? One because pre-1965 silver coins are 90% silver. They are sold today as "junk silver". They will make good barter because their value is less "dense" than gold coins; i.e., you can trade a dime or quarter (today) worth $2.00 and $5.00 respectively, better than a 1/10th ounce gold coin worth $180.00, and they will protect against inflation. Two, because the U.S. Government has confiscated gold and bullion in the past, and they can do it again. Why do I say silver first? Because the historical price ratio of 16 to 1 (gold price to silver) indicates silver at $35 per ounce is undervalued to gold's current market level of $1800 per ounce. With gold at $1800 per ounce, silver should be trading at around $112. Silver's upside is proportionately greater than gold's. So, if you choose coins to hedge the coming inflation, take possession of them and bury them or hide them somewhere safe in an airtight, waterproof, and decay proof containers.

And, while I'll get into caching later, it's always a good idea to have several caches of your precious metal assets. Never put all your eggs in one basket. When purchasing your coins, give the vendor from whom you purchase your metals as little personal information as possible. This is entirely legal as long as legal guidelines are followed and taxes are paid upon gains from sales. With only a handful of exceptions, I recommend getting most of your assets out of Dollar based investments!

The messenger of this catastrophe is already knocking at our door. The messenger is the (widely publicized) doom of the Euro and the EU's mad scramble to find a solution to keep it from collapsing altogether. Bailouts will prove to be short term stopgaps only; I strongly suspect there will be no stopping the Euro's demise. I don't believe it can be stopped, because the only way to do so, would be by some miracle of increasing not only the GDP of the failing countries, but to miraculously purchase the GDP of the failing countries back into prosperity. It could not happen in the next 12 months, and unlikely to happen in the next 12 years. I believe failure of the Euro is likely and as soon as the exchanges of currency are complete, the next dominos will fall, and the Dollar will be amongst them. The Dollar will collapse because there WILL be NO MORE foreign investment in U.S. Treasuries unless China's entire national economy is thrown into support of the Dollar. This is not going to happen; China is already hedging its losses, and China is not energy independent and must trade with the oil producing countries in the currency of choice. While "some" OPEC countries' choice may remain the Dollar due to political and military pressures, most OPEC countries, I believe, will favor other currencies (the Yuan, if China succeeds in placing it as the world reserve currency), or precious metals. Because the Dollar WILL be demonstrating devaluation, no government will want to hold as it declines. India is already moving toward purchasing its oil in gold, it has publicly stated so, and China, Russia, and other countries will follow.

Just like Greece, Italy, Spain, and Portugal, America does not produce enough GDP to sustain its $15.6 Trillion debt and the interest, and thus with the ceasing of foreign investment, the Dollar MUST follow the Euro into devaluation and possibly collapse. As for a time-line, the Euro must fail first, then perhaps other weaker currencies, and then the Dollar. We have perhaps two years or so, before an economic melt-down; probably less. Hyperinflation will accelerate the arrival.

The bottom line is, it is the debasement of the dollar and hyperinflation that will be the ultimate cause of the catastrophe we are about to experience. Whether it is a result of an international, financial chess game with China, an intentional debasement by our own government for the purposes of paying its staggering debt with cheaper dollars, or a middle east conflict locking up oil supplies, it is runaway inflation that will crumble our economy and result in a calamity.

While your cache of silver or gold coins might protect some of your financial assets against inflation, they could be of little value (beyond barter value) when considering your day to day survival. The focus of this booklet is on gaining a mindset to prepare for physical survival, not so much financial survival.

With many people already living on far less than just a few years ago, and many living on fixed incomes, the cost of goods will soar beyond reach. Gasoline for cars and diesel for trucks will become prohibitively expensive or altogether unavailable, the lumber yard and hardware stores won't be able to get lumber, hardware and tools. The baker won't be able to get flour, and the butcher won't be able to get his meat, and the list goes on ad infinitum. If the power grids are not already down, the electric company will ration power, the water and gas companies will be forced to limit service hours. Most industries and suppliers of commodities, including food producers, fuel refineries and distribution, and manufacturers of everything from building materials to pharmaceuticals will be forced to shut down and stop shipping. With demand rising and less to sell, retail outlets will eventually be forced to close and more jobs will be lost. As trade grinds to an abrupt halt, so too does spending. Slowing spending means others have less to spend and so goes the downward spiral. When spending ceases, tax revenues dry up and government services evaporate. And, this is when chaos and anarchy begin.

So how do we prepare? The first step is to trash the "normalcy bias" and anticipate the possibility of a catastrophe, and know... we will be responsible for ourselves, (hopefully to include) our "community", and vice versa. No one else will come to rescue us.

Survival preparation covers a broad spectrum. It can be total self-sufficiency at home, in a fortified, off-the-grid outpost with long term water supply, livestock, and feed and crop production, and the knowledge and means to process it all, or it can mean simply surviving the initial catastrophic days. While I will discuss long term survival later in this booklet, my initial focus will be on surviving the first few days or weeks.

Deciding to Bug Out Or Stay Put

I touched lightly on situations that may require bugging out and some that may not require bugging out. Ultimately, that decision is up to you, but there are some considerations that should be given to whether to grab your gear and git, or to stay put.

In an ideal world, where your preparations are already in place, you will have already headed out to your refuge and would stay put there. But, the ideal may not be realistically pragmatic, so my attention will be to heading out just before, at the time of, or shortly after the catastrophic event occurs.

Heading out to your refuge is an escape from dangerous situations you would face if you stayed at home. These will be dangerous times and either staying put, or heading out, you will face situations not faced before.

Heading out, however, is dangerous in itself. You WILL encounter problems in escape mode that you would not encounter on a summer drive. You will encounter others, in a panic, doing the same thing you're doing. You may encounter road blocks (by would-be robbers, police, or military), faked or staged accidents to get you to stop so you can be robbed, people tailing you to your destination, impassable roads, road rage, and a host of other situations that could seriously hinder your get-away, prevent it, or injure you. Bugging out should be considered when the danger you would face is greater if you stayed than if you didn't. While there are many reasons you might not be able to stay at home, here are a few (and there well could be others):

Hurricane
Flood
Volcanic eruption
Raging and unstoppable urban and suburban fires
Anarchy and uncontrollable lawlessness
Nuclear attack
Chemical or biological attack

Just because you have left for your refuge destination, doesn't mean you are safe. There will be others who have left for safety too, but may have not prepared to survive on the road or in a wilderness situation. When they find you, with all of your supplies, water, and food, you will be a likely target, just as if you had stayed at home. If your refuge is a makeshift encampment, you have lost whatever security your home may have offered.

Unless the calamity is an act of mother nature (hurricane, flood, volcanic eruption, or wildfire), or a nuclear, chemical, or biological attack, I would be a tough one to convince bugging out is the best option. Nevertheless, there are some serious considerations to be given to staying put.

Most apartments and homes today, provide easy access to any who would want to breach a window or door. In times of chaos and anarchy, the robbers and burglars aren't going to be the prowler or cat burglar types. They will be bold and forceful, probably armed, and with a kick, a brick, or heavy pipe will gain easy access to the inside of your home, you, your food, your money, and your guns and ammunition. Your home is vulnerable, unless you have barred your windows and doors, you have rollup and dropdown steel shutters on every window and opening, and you are totally self-contained and off grid, and this is unlikely. Fenced yards, barking dogs, and locked gates are no deterrent to a driven and desperate, would-be thief.

While a major earthquake may have made your home untenable and you might still be able to remain or camped close by, the biggest danger in my opinion is the high likelihood of persons going in search of food, fuel, guns, and ammunition. They will be thirsty, hungry, and desperate, and they will perpetrate crimes of everything from burglary and robbery to looting, and home invasion (including assault on you or your family). If they believe you are supplied to stay put (and they will, if you are staying put and not leaving like many), they will use any means necessary to get at what you have. They will drive cars through front rooms, they will throw Molotov cocktails in to burn and smoke you out, they will shut down your power or turn on all your water spigots and wait for you to come out. They will come as individuals, or marauding gangsters, or will pose as "friendly" neighbors or visitors, distressed victims running to you for safety, or even dressed as police officers, members of the military, or other first responders. There is no limit to the means and ways they will employ to get at your supplies.

With all of this to consider, your home may still be the best place to ride out the catastrophe. For one, you (most likely) live within a neighborhood or community. While I will discuss the benefits of community preparation later, I will say here that preparing to survive doom with your community is a must. The tribe is always more formidable than the individual.

Members of communities share work, supplies, food, water, and provide diversity in skill sets, and emotional comfort. There is always greater safety in numbers, and protecting the community is better achieved than protecting one residence. Community members can act as lookouts, scouts, and in numbers, as a militia of sorts. It would be a rather bold gang, indeed, that accosted multiple homes or dwellings in a community where a cohesive group of lookouts and defenders were prepared to receive them and meet them with equally aggressive boldness.

It is important to get your community to prepare. Most are not as likely to scoff at your plans as you might think. Some yes, they smirk at what they perceive as fanatical pessimism. Most, however, I believe are realistic and would support efforts to get the community more prepared to face unknown dangers. Those who don't care to participate may be the neighbors who come knocking at your door when the calamity arrives.

If you stay at home, identify a perpetual source of water. It could be a river, stream, lake, pond, well, or reservoir. And remember trips out for water or anything could subject you to risk. And, I recommend having a pull wagon, cart, or adult tricycle with baskets for carting water, wood, or whatever. You should have water stored at home. Keep 45 gallons (nine 5 gallon carboys) of water for every person in your household, if at all possible; use 1 or 2 gallon plastic containers, if the 5 gallon carboys are unmanageable for you. If the power goes down, don't flush the toilets or use up the hot water in your hot water tank; that is drinking water if water service goes out. Try to stock up on food for a minimum 6 months; better if a year. I will provide a full checklist of items for long term survival later.

If staying at home, you should seriously consider concealment. Black plastic to cover windows at night, automatic sprinklers off, no trash put out at curbside, etc. Concealed or camouflaged battery operated motion detector alarms are very good at letting you know someone is outside your home, and they're quite inexpensive (around $25.00 for a good one). Surveillance cameras are a good investment too, but make sure you have a battery powered system, as the power could be down, rendering it worthless. While you don't want your home to appear completely vacant, you want it to appear as no one is home. Why? Element of surprise for any would-be intruders. Take it from a cop, surprise is disconcerting, especially to those breaking in to what they thought was an empty house. The normal human reaction to surprise is to run away. Surprise can be a lot of things. The sound of a pump shotgun, cycling a round into the chamber is disconcerting; so is a big nasty dog with a deep growl and sharp white teeth. A firearm, fitted with a red laser beam sight, lighting the chest of an intruder is equally discontenting (for the intruder). I have my reservations about shooting just anyone, but if they are an immediate and imminent threat to you or another inside your home, and the threat is of severe bodily injury or death, you have a right to self defense and the defense of others. If the threat of marauding gangs and looters is imminent (and it will be when the calamity hits), have in place a two-way radio communication network up and working within your community, so help and backup is seconds away. While your home should appear "quiet" (or vacant), your community must know you are there. You must know which of your neighbors are present, as well.

So there you have it. Even though you might think you're prepared, these times are going to challenge us.

The Bug Out Bag

If you've decided you have to bug out, you'll need to have your gear ready to go. The Bug Out Bag (B.O.B.) is a short term solution. It's a backpack, a duffle bag, or a container that has basic supplies to see one through the first 72 hours following the initial event. FEMA refers to it as an earthquake kit, or storm kit. These are the same, however perhaps not centrally organized into a container to "grab and go", and within weight and space limits.

B.O.B.'s are not necessarily specific to a duration they must provide for. They can contain enough supplies to provide for 72 hours, or 30 or more days of survival, or they can be anywhere in between. A B.O.B. is typically the grab and go bag for the quick escape. The survival equipment list is nearly endless and the B.O.B.'s contents would be determined by the length of time one anticipates being in survival mode, and subject to practical weight and packing considerations. Consideration should be given to the geographic area in question, its climate and changing seasons, terrain, population, demographics, and infrastructure. In most situations, however, some basic items are essential and common to any B.O.B. The list may not include some items your circumstances could require, but it is a starting point, and hopefully thought provoking enough for you to consider other items you may want to include, or perhaps you'll feel you can exclude. Nothing is "set in concrete". You need to anticipate your needs and supply your B.O.B. accordingly, and I will try to help you with a checklist for reference. Before I get into the basic item "Check List", I will mention again, with emphasis, that you probably already have many items in your home, apartment, or garage that are considered essential. With a little searching and creativity, much of the cost of assembling a B.O.B. can be defrayed. What is most important about the B.O.B. is that is a consolidated package of survival gear ready for you to grab and go with, at a moment's notice.

Basic item "Check List" for a B.O.B. (you are probably not going to be able to get everything listed in a compact, lightweight B.O.B. Some specific items are absolutely essential; some you might get by without. While noting that inclusion of each individual item listed is not necessarily essential, addressing each "category", however, is essential.

A. Your "Plans": (which you have formulated well in advance; including notes, instruction manuals, <u>maps</u> and your written escape route(s). When considering your escape route(s) have a Plan B and Plan C, in case Plan A fails. Keep in mind, GPS may not be functional. And most of all, include your "experience, knowledge, and practice").

B. Water:
   ☐ 1 liter per day, minimum.
   ☐ water purification tablets
   ☐ bleach (3 drops per quart purifies water of biological contaminants)
   ☐ filter (ceramic or charcoal)
   ☐ portable distilling device
   ☐ extra water container.

C. Food:
   ☐ ration bars

☐ long shelf life prepared foods
☐ freeze dried foods
☐ dehydrated foods
☐ canned foods

D. Clothing and Personal Items (consider climatic conditions):
☐ underwear
☐ socks
☐ pants
☐ shirts
    NOTE: Clothing is a source of string, thread, and fiber. Clothing is suitable for additional bandages.
☐ belts
☐ jackets
☐ hats
☐ gloves
☐ shoes
☐ boots
☐ rain poncho
☐ glasses, reading glasses, sun glasses
☐ magnifying glass (you can see splinters and stingers with it, and it can start a fire by magnifying and focusing direct sunlight)
☐ cell phone (may or may not work)

- [ ] binoculars, telescope,
- [ ] watches
- [ ] calculator (solar or battery operated)
- [ ] rucksack or backpack (if not the container itself)
- [ ] Umbrella (camouflaged fabric)
- [ ] walking stick (of stout hardwood, 5' to 6' in length; this is a self defense item as much as it is for walking)
- [ ] writing materials (pens and pencils)
- [ ] ruler
- [ ] notebook
- [ ] divider compass
- [ ] lensatic sighting compass
- [ ] camera (even though digital computer may not be available, camera can still record events)
- [ ] towel (hand and face)
- [ ] detergent (small bottle)
- [ ] handi-wipes, baby wipes
- [ ] toilet paper
- [ ] camp chair or stool

E. Shelter, sleeping, and comforts:

- [ ] House, ranch house, outpost, boat, RV, tent, or tarp etc.

- [ ] creature comforts (sleeping bag, blankets, cot, and pad - if space is available)

F. Special medications:

- [ ] prescription drugs (pack enough for an extended period of time as they may be unavailable for long periods)
- [ ] lotions
- [ ] insect repellent, Deet
- [ ] sun block lotion
- [ ] vitamins and nutrients

G. First Aid Kit (high quality):

- [ ] bandages (variety strip type)
- [ ] butterfly bandages
- [ ] adhesive tape (narrow to wide and ample length)
- [ ] gauzes
- [ ] self-adhesive wrap ("Ace" bandage)
- [ ] anti-bacterials (Betadine, iodine, isopropanol alcohol, and peroxide).
- [ ] Scissors
- [ ] tweezers
- [ ] surgical blade

- ☐ magnifying glass (second time mentioned - can't stress it enough)
- ☐ analgesics, pain killers
- ☐ suture kit

H. Essential Tools:

- ☐ combat knife (high quality, full tang)
- ☐ hatchet (if space is available)
- ☐ waterproof matches
- ☐ steel-magnesium strike match
- ☐ fire starter pellets (or bottle mineral spirits for fire starting)
- ☐ LED flashlight (high quality using AAA or AA batteries)
- ☐ mini lantern
- ☐ headlamp (AAA or AA battery powered
- ☐ rechargeable batteries (sizes for all electrical items)
- ☐ small solar battery charger (for batteries for all battery sizes your equipment requires)
- ☐ P38 or P51 can opener
- ☐ Leatherman tool
- ☐ trowel
- ☐ folding shovel

- ☐ small coil bailing wire
- ☐ parachute cord (minimum 50' hank)
- ☐ nylon string (225' roll)
- ☐ reflective tape (engineer's tape)
- ☐ folding saw (11" pruning saws work well - the cable or hand chain saws, I have found to be worthless; they are clumsy and become dull quickly)
- ☐ 3 road flares
- ☐ fence pliers (AKA fence tool)
- ☐ tarp
- ☐ leather gloves (can't stress importance of gloves enough)
- ☐ wax candle (not for the light, but for the wax; good lubricant, and melted over paper or dry sticks makes excellent fire starter)
- ☐ signal mirror
- ☐ laser pointer (high powered or "laser rescue flare" - they're expensive, but can cast a bright beam of light for many miles)
- ☐ duct tape.

I. Kitchen and cooking utensils:

- ☐ camp set fork-knife-spoon

- ☐ 2 qt. aluminum pot
- ☐ aluminum drinking cup
- ☐ reusable plastic or aluminum plate and bowl
- ☐ water bucket (collapsible)
- ☐ backpack stove (or other suitable cooking device; debris burning woodsman's stoves are great in that they require no special fuel)
- ☐ fuel for stove (if conventional backpacking stove)
- ☐ triangle can and bottle opener (with cork screw)

J. Self Defense:

- ☐ Firearms
- ☐ appropriate ammunition (quantity and caliber)
- ☐ taser
- ☐ pepper spray
- ☐ knives
- ☐ clubs or batons (you can make these)
- ☐ hatchets
- ☐ spears (you can make these)
- ☐ bows and arrows
- ☐ crossbows and bolts

☐ your "knowledge of how to make" traps, snares, and pitfalls.

*Before you go bragging about how you're going to blow away someone whom you think is going to harm you or steal your cache, or before you go out and buy an arsenal of weapons to defend yourself and family or your cache, you need to consider the impact of severely injuring someone or taking someone's life. The consequences for such a defensive act could be, in themselves, catastrophic to you, your family, the perpetrator-victim, and the perpetrator-victim's family in more ways than can be counted. Your self-defense, and the defense of other human life against imminent severe bodily injury or death is one thing, but defense of a few food items or a can of gasoline is another. Don't take it casually. YOUR victim may be a good person, just hungry and desperate. You may consider protection of your shelter, food, and water supply (or shortage thereof) to be vital to your survival, or the survival of your family, and therefore justify the use of force (deadly or otherwise). This is a determination only you can make. Employ wisdom when you make it.

K. Communications:

☐ radios (FRS/GMRS, HAM, CB, AM-FM)
☐ Short Wave-Weather radio (solar powered, hand cranked, and battery operated emergency radios are a good investment).

L. Cash and Barter Items:

☐ cash (may be of declining value, but it wouldn't hurt to have some already in your bug out bag - small denomination coins, bills)
☐ cigarettes
☐ small bottles of Vodka or other liquor
☐ chocolate bars or candy
☐ ration bars or nutrition bars
☐ coffee and sugar, powder drink mixes
☐ matches (boxes of)
☐ lighters
☐ magnifying glasses (to see with; to start fires with)
☐ pocket knives

☐ extra pairs gloves

M. Pets:

☐ dog, cat, rabbit, or whatever (don't leave them behind or without care)
☐ pet food (take ample food and water for your pet)
☐ dish (feeding and watering dish)
☐ leash (or restraint)
☐ collar with I.D. (embedded I.D. chips may be useless if scanners and power are out)

Bugging Out

While some may plan to bug out on foot, or on a bicycle, for most people, bugging out will mean taking off to safety in a motor vehicle. Some may have a motorcycle, some may have a quad, some may plan on leaving in a boat. Whatever means you choose, the same basics of preparation apply. For purposes of this discussion, I will refer to a conventional motor vehicle.

In a bug out situation, driving on paved highways may be impossible, or dangerous for a variety of reasons. You may have to travel roads less traveled and that may mean back roads or off road driving.

For the well experienced off road enthusiast there may be a very fine line between survival mode and recreation. If the excursions taken by off roaders are many, extensive, and diverse, they have already encountered situations requiring experience, ingenuity, and the right equipment; they know how to make it on their own. For them, it's as much recreation as it is survival. But for the recreationist whose definition of recreation is 18 holes on a POSH golf course, or sitting on the fantail of a chartered yacht, sipping a margarita, there is a distinct and bold line between survival mode and recreation. Most of us, however fall somewhere in between.

The experienced and equipped off roader already knows what to carry and how to use it, so my vehicle and travel prep lists are attuned more to those who don't quite have that level of experience.

Always keep your vehicle in good repair.

Vehicle Checklist:

- ☐ oil (have it changed regularly)
- ☐ tires (make sure they are in good condition and properly inflated
- ☐ lubrication (make sure the joints and fittings are properly and recently lubricated.
- ☐ jack (make sure you have a jack (preferably a "high lift" jack)
- ☐ lug wrench (good "cross" wrench is best)

- ☐ spare tire (make sure it's in good shape and inflated)
- ☐ fuel (always keep your vehicle fueled. Never let it get below 1/2 tank so it's ready to get away. Fuel might not be available, or lines at the gas station may be prohibitively long and jammed with people trying to get fuel to get out of town. I will discuss caching of items later, but consider caching fuel within a range reachable by your vehicle when the tank is half full
- ☐ tire repair kit (this can be anything from a plug and glue kit, to inside-the-tire patches with heat glue, and tire irons and rim/tire removal spoons). For most situations, the plug and glue kit will suffice
- ☐ small air compressor, 12 volt battery powered, with cigarette lighter adapter
- ☐ 2 gallons extra fuel (or, if capable, extra jerry cans of fuel)
- ☐ extra motor oil
- ☐ filler hose and/or funnel
- ☐ Siphon tube (min. 48" long)
- ☐ 2 gallons water (or, if capable extra carboys or jerry cans of water)

- ☐ tube JB Weld (sealant), and tube of silicone sealant
- ☐ consider: Mobile CB radio and/or 10 Meter Ham (sideband) mounted in your vehicle. This would be in addition to the FRS/GMRS radios packed in your B.O.B.
- ☐ automotive tool kit (socket wrenches, open and box wrenches, pliers, screw drivers, allen wrenches, etc.)
- ☐ rubber hose repair tape and stainless hose clamps
- ☐ fan belt or serpentine belt (extra)
- ☐ chain with hooks, cable with hooks, or tow strap with hooks
- ☐ jumper cables
- ☐ shovel
- ☐ road flares (box of 12)
- ☐ triangular reflectors
- ☐ fire extinguisher (category ABC)
- ☐ hand degreaser
- ☐ shop towels
- ☐ whisk broom / wire brush
- ☐ tarp or ground cover and blanket
- ☐ 16" X 16" square of plywood, 1 1/8" thick (2-4-1 subfloor product), or 2

Pcs. 3/4" 16" X 16" plywood, face glued together.

☐ 16 pcs. of 2" X 4" 18" long, wood blocks (hardwood if possible).

About the plywood... I was reading a popular survival manual. The author suggested carrying an airbag to inflate with the exhaust pipe to raise the car when changing a tire or stuck in soft sand. While the manual is packed with other valuable information, I almost had to believe this author had never done much off roading. For one thing, trying to seal a bag around an exhaust pipe to achieve the degree of inflation necessary to support a car or truck, could prove difficult, if not impossible. Second, where does one find such a bag that won't melt or burn when in contact with a hot exhaust pipe? Third, how does one keep from puncturing it on sharp gravel or steel auto-underbody parts? And fourth, how does one place it sufficiently under a car that is buried to its axles, to raise it? Possible, I guess, but not very pragmatic. I have been stuck in the sand or had to change a tire in soft sand on too many off road excursions to even remember. I always carry a thick piece of 16" square plywood; it works wonderfully as a base to place under the jack (boards crack; thick plywood doesn't).

About the blocks... I always carried a bundle of 16 pcs. The 2X4 blocks pack nicely into a 4 pc. X 4 pc. bundle (6" high X 14" wide X 18" long) and they come in very handy as "tread" under a tire, when stuck. Many times, I've jacked up my truck, filled in the hole the spinning tire made, laid down the blocks in tread-like fashion, and driven away from the hole. Don't forget to collect up the blocks and don't burn them up in your campfire. They're more valuable as tread than as firewood. I have also "crossed cribbed" them to make a sturdy jack-stand support 12" high. They're certainly not high tech, but just come in handy as heck sometimes.

Avoid soft sand, and mud, if you do not have 4 wheel drive (sometimes, even if you do), and experience driving in it. I was on an off road expedition once along a very remote beach in the south-central part of Baja California. One member of our party took his 4 wheel drive truck out onto the wet sand, where the tide had gone out. Within seconds, his truck had sunken in the mud all the way to the door sills and was continuing to sink deeper. His 4 wheel drive was worthless and no amount of digging could have saved him. Were it not for our other two trucks with heavy duty winches, his truck would have soon joined another SUV that was rolling around in the surf. The moral here is, don't go where you don't know how your vehicle is going to handle the surface consistency of the terrain (or how the terrain is going to handle your vehicle). If you are unsure, stop, get out and slowly walk the surface to find out what it is and what it will do. Had my friend done this, he would have found himself up to his knees in quick sand, but he would have been much easier to pull out than his truck was. If you don't have 4 wheel drive, and high clearance, avoid rough, rocky, or uneven terrain. I've encountered more than a few newer, crossover SUV's, with 4 wheel drive, high centered and stuck on rocks, or arroyo embankments because they didn't have the ground clearance to get over the obstacle. The moral here is, don't drive in terrain that your vehicle can't handle or in terrain where you have no experience. Simply put, you will find yourself stuck, and you will have created an additional distressful or dangerous situation that could have been avoided. If you need experience, get it before the bug out.

The B.O.B. and the above items can fit into the trunks of most cars. In getting prepared, you will find out now and not wait until the moment when you have to bug out. If you're lucky cnough to have a pickup truck (better yet... a 4 wheel drive pickup truck), the entire list of vehicle items (except the extra fuel and water... depending on how much you carry) can fit easily into a decent sized, lockable, pickup tool box. With a pickup, you might even want to expand on the items in the "Essential tools" category. The rest of the pickup bed can be used for your other camping gear, cots, coolers, tables, chairs, tent, firewood and lighter fluid, bicycles, or whatever. If you're at this level, I'm not telling you anything you don't already know.

Bugging out should include a community of people and vehicles; if possible, don't bug out alone.

Where To Go?

Unless you have a ranch, outpost, family with a farm, or out-of-the-way Inn within a reasonable distance, you need to identify your hideout, how far you'll have to travel, and how you're going to get there. Getting prepared to escape a catastrophe is only one small part of the prepping-to-survive itinerary. Many people think about bugging out and many people stock up on the survival items to do it, but have given little thought to how and where they're going, or whether they are staying put. Unless you have Plan A, with Plan B and Plan C backups for bugging out, your (well intended, but limited) preparation may be of little use.

Few people have survived more than 4 or 5 days without water. Remember the essentials for sustaining life; water, food, and shelter. Even though your bug out bag will include water for surviving a few days (or weeks if you've loaded up the back of your pickup truck, or the tanks in your RV), you will need to find a refuge that has a source of water. Fresh water can be found as city tap water, a well, a spring, a river, a stream, lake, reservoir, pond, or any area with ample year round rainfall. If you have a functional distilling system, or reverse osmosis filter, even the ocean can provide the source for your water. A tarp was recommended (twice) as an essential item for your bug out bag, not just because it can provide shelter or ground cover, but because a tarp is a good rainwater collection device.

In that one may not know the duration of the effects of the calamity, one should at least prepare for weeks, if not months. In identifying your hideout, a source of water should be the first consideration. Perhaps your own home is the best bug out hideout. You probably have city water service (unless you have a private well), but the power may go out, and then you won't have any replenishable water from conventional sources. Nevertheless, you will have some water for a time; the water you stored, the water in your toilet tank(s), hot water heater, perhaps in a swimming pool, spa, a nearby reservoir, or stream or river, but in any case you must have water. If you are forced to leave your home, you need to identify a location with a good source of water, and (conveniently) it is there you most likely will find some of your long term food needs are met as well. If your source of water is city tap water that is not likely to be toxic and it still flows, then your bug out hideout might be a motel, hotel, or Inn in some out of the way place, but it may not be an ecosystem supporting potential food sources, either.

Your bug out may be quick and necessitate a hideout in the outdoors, so you're going to have to find a location with water. Most non-toxic bodies of water attract wildlife, and support some foliage. Most bodies of water, except some wells and springs support aquatic life of some kind, also.

If you're going to end up outdoors, when deciding on your location, make sure there is no source of pollution affecting the water. Springs can be polluted by chemicals, salts, minerals, lead, and other pollutants that can be present naturally, or come from industrial sources, such as chemical plants, refineries, and mining operations. Before bug out time and when doing your scouting, take water samples and get them tested if you can. Biological pollutants can more easily be removed than chemical or mineral pollutants. Boiling fresh water for 8 or more minutes, at sea level, or 13 or more minutes at 8,000' (water boils at a lower temperature at higher altitudes) will kill 99% of biological pollutants. I have heard some people say the water only need reach a temperature of 147 degrees for 5 minutes. That's a minimum and why chance it? Boil it for 8 minutes! Boiling usually does not remove any chemical or mineral pollutants, but merely increases the density and contamination level. Distilling, on the other hand, removes all pollutants (however, some solvents boil at a lower temperature than water and thus your distilling, while boiling, should include allowing vapor to exit for a few minutes before connecting to the condenser). Ordinary household liquid bleach or Iodine tablets cure most of the biological pollution, but do nothing to remove chemical pollutants. A good ceramic or charcoal filter, may remove all biological pollutants and some chemical pollutants. Rivers or streams with no upstream polluters are usually safe sources, if you filter or boil your water. Lakes usually provide cleaner water than ponds, simply because they are larger, support convection currents (moving the water) and dilute the pollutants more. Moving water, or larger bodies of water where the wind aerates the water, are much better than standing or stagnant water. Motorized boating traffic is a polluter of water, and where it occurs gasoline and oil are pollutants. A good filter or distillation is recommended. Whatever the case, make your hideout location one where the water is as good as you can find. But, I need to add a word of caution. I once canoed the Colorado River from Hoover Dam to Lake Mojave. There are a number of hot springs along the river. Some of the hot springs were known to harbor dangerous viruses. While hot springs may have potable water, I would not recommend drinking water from a hot spring, unless you know it to be safe. Likewise, some lakes and ponds support toxic algae. Make sure you boil, distill, or filter your water.

Keep in mind, that bodies of water support entire ecosystems. Plant life and wildlife are part of the system. The ecosystem is home to plants, insects and other critters, which are a food source for yet other creatures. Some critters, from the tiny insects to the larger animals, may prove irritating or even dangerous to you. Above the aquatic life in the body of water, don't be surprised to find everything from stinging flies and mosquitoes, to worms, centipedes, scorpions, spiders, amphibians, reptiles (including venomous snakes), rodents, fowl, felines, canines, antlered and horned grazers and foragers, and so on... up the food chain. And, with knowledge, caution, and preparation, you get to be at the top of the food chain.

Foliage can be edible. It provides shade, fire fuel, or materials to make shelter. I won't go into what is edible and what is not with regard to plant life, but there are numerous good books on the subject to help you identify what is edible and what is not. I will only add the caveat that some plants are highly toxic, even lethal, when eaten or even burned (if you inhale the smoke); so do your homework after scouting locations and determine what is edible and what is not, and if you don't know whether a plant is toxic or not, assume it is and don't eat it.

Most wildlife, if properly prepared, is edible. I have not been a serious large game hunter, however I have done some, and as a deputy sheriff in wilderness areas, I spent considerable time in hunting camps, checking game tags, game limits, hunting licenses, firearms regulation compliance, and observing game preparation. Although somewhat different, the preparation for larger animals versus smaller animals, the skinning, gutting, and process for jointing or sectioning meat, is pretty straightforward. Fowl only needs gutting, plucking, and rinsing. Like the edible plants, I won't go into game preparation, or cooking it. There are many good books on the subject and they should not only be part your preparation library, they should be included in your B.O.B.

You now know the importance of finding a bug out hideout with a source of water; it offers water, food, and foliage for building shelter and concealment. Finding one that lends protection from adverse climate and weather, and concealment add another dimension to the task. Woodlands, grasslands, swamplands, and deserts are vastly different and each adds a different dimension to the aquatic ecosystem. If you live in a region where forests are abundant, then most likely you will establish your hideout in a forest. If you live in the southwest, then your hideout will most likely be in a desert region, unless you retreat to a higher elevation... and so on.

Now is a good time to refer back to your essential tools list. If in a swampy area, you will need to add a machete to your list of tools. If you retreat to a forest, you might want to give more thought to the saw you choose, than someone headed for the desert. If headed for the desert, protection from the sun is important, and if you find yourself in a grassland, protection from the wind and exposure to storms may be more important to you. These are the anticipation considerations I've referred to, and will continue to refer to throughout this book. Scout out your retreat, and know it well, and what essentials will be required BEFORE you have to bug out.

Finding protection from weather, climate, and terrain dangers is a consideration to be taken seriously. During a 4 wheel driving excursion in Baja, we were taking a break along a dry arroyo. We (fortunately) had parked our vehicles atop the embankment and not down in the dry bed itself. It was a warm spring day, and there was not a cloud in the sky, except off in the distance over the mountains to our west. We heard a rumbling sound coming from up the creek bed and within just a few seconds, a literal wall of water, 7' or 8' high came rushing down the arroyo. I have seen flash flooding before, but never quite so dramatic as this. It brought home the power and surprise mother nature can deliver without warning. One minute, the arroyo was a dry, tranquil sandy and rocky stream bed. The next minute, it was a raging whitewater river that would have washed our trucks and bodies all the way to the Sea of Cortez. It is imperative when selecting your bug out encampment, you consider all the elements nature can throw at you. Cliffs might offer good wind protection, but falling rocks and mudslides can kill. Conifer forests may offer concealment, clean water, fire fuel, and wind protection, but may be a dangerous place in a heavy electrical storm. Large conifers are lightning rods, especially if rooted (and grounded) in or around rock outcroppings. Once while backpacking in the Sierra Nevada, I was camped just off the trail, near a large granite outcropping, trying to stay dry in the downpour, when a lightning bolt hit a nearby pine and literally splintered the tree into a pile of toothpicks.

On another occasion in late winter in Colorado, I was on patrol, in a 4 wheel drive pickup truck, in a very remote part of the back country along the front range and I decided to patrol-check a road that was closed in winter. There was some snow still on the road, but a supervisor in the county maintenance yard had told me they had plowed the road a few days earlier. As I proceeded down the road and down a rather steep incline, and into a more heavily treed area, the snow in the shadows of the trees had not melted off as much and it became increasingly deeper and more icy. Thinking the yard had plowed as they had told me, I continued on around a bend only to find a bank of snow 10' high, blocking the road, where the plow had stopped. I turned the truck around and began to head back only to find the hill I had just come down was too steep, too deep in slushy snow and ice for the 4 wheel drive to climb. I was one of the lucky ones, as I was able to radio the yard to send a tow truck and a grader plow to get me out. Many people have not had such luck, and have become victims of being stranded in a remote area in the freezing cold, or equally, in blistering hot, arid regions, and out of cell phone range. What had I failed to observe? While the supervisor had told me the road had been plowed a few days earlier, it clearly had not. There had been no snowfall for a couple of weeks, and I should have noted before I headed down the road, that the supervisor must have either misunderstood which road I was going to take, or one of the plow drivers had misinformed him. The road had not been recently plowed and I should have taken note of the road's condition before I started down, rather than just assume what the supervisor told me was correct. My illustrations here are to highlight the dangers in not observing the subtle signs, and anticipating the worst case scenario for the terrain, climate, and weather conditions.

When selecting your hideout encampment, whether it be a waypoint on your trek to your final hideout, or the final hideout itself, it is highly important to consider all the elements mother nature has in her bag of surprises. Ravines and arroyos are not good places to set up camp. The immediate edges of rivers and streams are not good places because water levels can change in minutes. Rivers, streams, or outlets downstream from reservoirs are frequently subject to quick rising water, as outflows constantly change. The base of cliffs are not good places, and sparsely treed areas around rock outcroppings, during electrical storms, are not good places either. While you're taking note of the terrain, note animal paths as well. Animals travel between their own dens or hideouts, or feeding range, and water. Some animals are dangerous. I live at the foot of the Santa Ana Mountains in Southern California. The mountains are home to an abundance of wildlife including snakes, rabbit, squirrel, deer, fox, raccoon, goat, javelina, coyote, bear, bobcat, and mountain lion. In the news every so often, we hear of a mountain biker, or hiker who was attacked and killed, right in our own backyard by a mountain lion. Animals must be considered when determining your hideout.

While venomous snakes are found all over the United States, having spent a great deal of time in the desert regions of the southwest and Mexico, I feel the need to mention the dangers of rattlesnakes. Among other species of rattlesnakes, the Mojave (Green) Rattlesnake (Crotalus Scutulatus) should be noted for its particularly potent venom. While most rattlesnake venoms possess a hemotoxin, the venom of the Mojave Rattlesnake contains a neurotoxin as well. While no rattlesnake bite should be (nor will it be) taken lightly, the Mojave Rattlesnake is deadly. The range of this snake is from New Mexico to the deserts of California, including Nevada, Arizona, and northern Mexico. Rattlesnakes are ambush predators and lie in wait for their prey to pass by. They are so well hidden and camouflaged (by their natural patterns and coloring) that they can be especially hard to see. One time while working mounted patrol in a large regional park in Southern California, my partner told me of a snake he saw coiled just off the side of the trail ahead of me. I looked and stared for several moments and still could not see the snake, nor did my horse see or smell it. Finally, when it moved, without a single rattle of its tail, I did see it and was able to avoid riding past it. My caution here is, be extra alert when walking in grassy or brushy areas, as many times a rattlesnake will not rattle, and you could be an unwary victim. Be sure you are wearing boots and clothing that are appropriate for the region, and with consideration to the critters you may encounter. When climbing in rocky areas, don't put your hands where you cannot see.

Fire is another consideration. The Santa Ana Mountains, and countless regions around America, are very frequently, hit with raging brush, timber, or grass, fires, fanned by hurricane force winds. Needless to say, a wildfire moving at 25 miles per hour, cannot be outrun. Unless you're O.K. with being a piece of burnt toast, be certain your hideout is not in heavy undergrowth, old dead standing timber, or parched long grass, and is not subject to an extremely dry, high wind fire season.

Bugging out doesn't mandate that your destination is one specific location, either. You may decide a nomadic bug out is safer than landing in one spot and staying put. Bugging out is putting yourself into survival mode: get out of the way of (avoid), or protect yourself from the harm confronting you. Off road enthusiasts often hit the trail with only a generalized region to explore. They are effectively nomadic, traveling from point A to point B, to point C, and so on until they return home, or their base of operations. But, I know of few off roaders who would head out without at least a set of topographical maps of the area(s) they're headed in to, and a decent lensatic compass. So if you decide your bug out is going to be nomadic, don't leave your travel to wandering. Know the area, and have maps of the area you will travel.

Changing one's encampment daily, or every few days, accomplishes a couple of valuable objectives. It familiarizes you with the terrain, climate, and weather better than staying at one location. It may (and usually does) expose you to resources you may not have known about or encountered had you remained in one location. It also can make you more elusive, and that may be a very real and primary concern, but it can (and probably will) mean you are more likely to encounter other people, and that might not be good. So the bottom line is, if you go "nomadic" you'll want to travel discreetly and have scouted your route with forward scouts who can radio back information, before making your entire party vulnerable to exposure to, or attack from others.

If you decide to stay on-the-go, replenish your water from your base source, head out, and return when needed, or, identify another such source along your route(s). If you choose to be nomadic in your bug out, remember you can cache water and fuel, beforehand, within your travel region.

I will mention caching here (and again in more detail later) as a means of assuring your supply of water, food, fuel, and other essentials. If you are traveling from Point A to Point B, in a more or less linear direction, you can place caches along your route to replenish supplies. If you have chosen to be nomadic within a specific geographical region, and intend to more or less remain within that area, you of course would strategically place your caches within that region, whatever it may be, or however large it may be. I have done off road caching when 4 wheeling, and I have cached in the Sierras when backpacking. When carrying your supplies, either by vehicle or on your back, and you travel far enough and/or stay long enough, eventually you will exhaust them. Caching in advance helps to avoid running out of supplies.

If I haven't scared you out of bugging out altogether, I hope I've impressed upon you the importance of selecting your encampment(s) and your supply maintenance with every consideration you have at your disposal.

Getting There

Once you've planned where you are going, you need to plan how you're going to get there. While some people are considering bugging out by hiking, bicycling, motorcycle, quad, or boat, I strongly suspect most people planning a possible bug out, are going to go by motor vehicle; or at least try to go by motor vehicle. You have your car or truck fueled up, your bug out bag, food and supplies are packed, you have your jerry can with extra gasoline, your water bottles are full, your cooler is full of beer and ice, and you're ready to hit it.

And hit it you do! You hit the freeway parking lot, with hundreds of thousands of cars and trucks all trying to get out of town just like you are, and all are at a near dead stop. Unless you live in a rural area, this is exactly what you will encounter. If you live in an urban or suburban area and ever tried to get out of town on Friday afternoon, before a holiday weekend, you have tasted what I'm referring to, and the larger the metropolitan area you live in or near, the worse it will be.

During the first few days and hours before Katrina was to hit the coast, people who had the faculties to decide to escape, but only did so at the last minute, faced a traffic jam that ran the entire length of the State of Louisiana. As the landfall hour approached, it took motorists as much as 10 hours to travel just 1 mile; that is not what I would call a successful escape. Many people, although out of the way of the flood waters, rode out the violence of the hurricane in their cars, stuck in traffic, on the roadway. Some on bicycles or motorcycles made it much further, but what they could bring was limited. Many left pets behind, and families got separated. Many who bugged out by bicycle or motorcycle found themselves victims of the elements anyway. Those who heeded landfall warnings of Hurricane Katrina and drove to safety more than 36 or 48 hours before the estimated landfall, not only encountered much less traffic, but found accommodations along the way.

So when bug out time arrives, what is one to do? Hopefully by now, you know the answer. It was to prepare early. That doesn't necessarily mean bug out earlier (but it should mean exactly that, if you know the catastrophe is coming), it means having anticipated the obstacles before it is time to move out. I can draw a parallel here having trained thoroughly as a law enforcement officer. Hesitation can be a killer. When scenarios are thoroughly practiced, much hesitation is eliminated. A police officer may have only a fraction of a second to act in self defense. If he hesitates, it may cost him his life. But, there is another side to this coin. Hesitation may save the wasting of a life, too. If you have practiced, like the officer, you will "read the situation" and your response will be second nature. That is the essence of the "split second decision" an officer (or you) must be able to make.

While on patrol one summer evening in Colorado, I was enroute from one open space area to another, when a call came out, "Shots fired behind the trading post on county road 120, units available?" I responded (with my call sign and 10-97) that I was passing the trading post at that moment. I drove past the trading post (as I was literally right in front of it) and circled back, stopping my unit about 75 yards south, and against a rock embankment. I walked up along the embankment and to the rear of the trading post, but found no one at the back of the trading post. With weapon drawn, of course, I entered the rear of the trading post and looked down the aisle directly at the clerk behind the counter. His body language suggested there was nothing unusual going on, so I asked him if there was any kind of disturbance. He said, "No", and inquired why I was there. I explained to him that I'd received a call that there had been shots fired in the vicinity and asked him if he had heard any gunfire. He said, no he hadn't. Meanwhile, my packset (handheld radio) wasn't powerful enough to broadcast down the canyon to the repeater that everything was code 4 (O.K.). Since I couldn't reach dispatch and tell them that everything was code 4, they had darn near the whole county rolling code 3 (red lights and siren) toward the trading post. The first deputy to arrive told me the house way up the hill had had previous dispatches regarding gunfire. So the both of us went back to the road leading up the hillside to that house. When we arrived, we saw a man and woman standing on the back porch. The man was holding a semi-auto pistol and the woman had an assault rifle. From the cover of our cars, and at a distance of about 150 feet, we told the couple to put down their weapons. They did not respond and pointed their weapons randomly about as though they were looking for a target. On several occasions, both pointed their weapons at the other officer and me. What kept me from shooting was their eyes never lined up with the direction their guns were pointing in; the gun would point one way, while the eyes would be staring off in another. The story goes on and it ended with no one getting hurt. We discovered later, the couple had been loaded on Methamphetamine and were paranoid. The point I want to make is, hesitation might be the right action to take. I could have legally fired in self-defense, but I didn't because I "read the situation".

"Reading the situation" is necessary regarding when to bug out, too. In a manner of speaking, when it's time to bug out, signals will buzz, alarms will sound, bells will ring, and lights will flash. If the catastrophe that I think will happen, happens, the news will announce the failure of the

Euro, and shortly thereafter, Congress will hold emergency budget meetings, the FED will be holding Congressional meetings, and politicians will assure us everything is copacetic; it's business as usual. But, we will see the price of commodities, including fuel, begin to rise sharply (even more than it already has). Banks could begin to close, interest rates will take overnight hikes, and access to cash might become limited or impossible. It will not be business as usual. These are the early warning signs. Your planning and preparation had better be done by this time. The time to jump in the car and head out, is when the grocery store shelves first start to empty out and gasoline stations begin to run out of fuel and close up. If you're on top of your game at this crucial time, you probably will be just ahead of the stampede, if that's where you want to be, OR this is where hesitation might be appropriate, but only if you have prepared. A good strategy in my opinion (if the catastrophe is not a storm, fire, or nuclear blast), may be to let the stampede run, wait (vigilantly) two or three days, let the mad rush die out, and then head out, taking back roads wherever possible, or decide to stay put, altogether.

If you decide to bug out, a good escape plan includes identification of all viable routes to your bug out area. You should not only know how to get where you are going, but be able to change course or routes, while enroute, that will still land you at your bug out destination, or planned cache site. This is not something to do when the "you know what" hits the fan. You must drive your routes. You must know where you can change roads, paths, or head off road, but still remain heading toward your bug out destination. This must be practiced, just like practicing with your equipment. It's all part of the same planning operation.

If the catastrophe is one of the other previously mentioned, the time to bug out will be when the government is caught by as much surprise as the public. Gas stations will run out of gasoline, store shelves will empty out, power may be out... effectively, things will deteriorate very quickly, and you may or may not get word the "have-nots" are on their way to take from the "haves"; when those who didn't prepare for disaster, go out to steal from those who did prepare. A catastrophe is almost always a surprise; that's why it's essential to PREPARE.

Caching

If bugging out by motor vehicle, even with a full tank of gasoline, you may not be able to reach your bug out destination. It could be too far to reach on a full tank, or it could be you burned far more fuel than you anticipated, just sitting in traffic for hours on your way out.

Caching is placing in hidden locations, any extra supplies you may need, including fuel, water, food, and equipment. When deciding where to place your caches, you should identify locations that will be along your route of travel and reachable in worst case scenarios; like when you thought you could get there on a full tank of gas, but you burned more gas than you thought you would, and now you only have a half tank to get there. Or, it's pouring rain, or snowing heavily and you cached your supplies up a canyon that is now a river or three feet deep in snow.

Deciding on where and how to cache requires a lot of consideration and planning. While you may not be able to avoid every possible situation that could arise, you can minimize complications in getting to your cache with the same practice of anticipation I've mentioned here again, and again.

When planning where to stash your cache, there are myriad variables to consider. Some you can know, and obviously some you simply cannot anticipate or have control over. But, here are some of the things to consider you can control:

- ☐ Distance from location of last supply source
- ☐ Good concealment, and protection from the elements
- ☐ Reliably being able to find it
- ☐ Practicality in getting there and (relatively) easy access
- ☐ Physical attributes or drawbacks of terrain (is it subject to flash flooding, vulnerable to wildfire, too visible, too difficult to access, routes there subject to flooding or closure, etc?)
- ☐ Is it public land or is it private land and do you have a right to be there, or will your being there constitute trespass?

What you may not be able to control are:

How long your cache may be there before you access it

The weather (and terrain) conditions at the time you want to access it, whether it has been discovered and taken, or if there are people there, or following you when you arrive to access it.

Never allow yourself to get so low on fuel, water, food, and supplies that you find yourself in a dire emergency situation should you not be able to reach, or find your cache. Always have enough reserve to extract yourself from the direness of an emergency. Pilots always carry enough fuel on board, so if a landing at the destination airstrip is not possible, they can make it to an alternate landing site. Your planning should be equally diligent.

In selecting your cache sites, try to put them within the distance your vehicle could travel on say... 3/8ths of a tank of fuel. Most vehicles will make 250 miles or so on a tank of fuel. So your cache sites need to be spaced something like 95 miles apart. This may seem like it's going to end up in excessive caching, but I believe it's better to have more supply, in shorter distances, than not enough. Now, take a good reliable map (either topographic or road map) and using a divider compass, from the scale of miles, draw radii at 95 mile intervals to rough out the areas where you can place caches.

Now you're going to have to make a drive, with your supplies to cache. You want to take your map (topographic and road maps; you can take your GPS for coordinate readings, but don't plan on relying on it because GPS may go down with the catastrophic event), your lensatic compass, divider compass, keeping track of your odometer reading from Point A to Point B, and so on, and head out toward your first area (presumably Point B). When you reach the general vicinity, make notes of, and take photos of the terrain (whenever possible, I take a paper plate and with a felt marker put a "B" on it (or B1, B2, B3, etc.), or whatever cache site it's going to be and get it in the photo so I know what site the photo refers to). Make special note of the geographic points of reference (it may be a mountain top with an unusually rocky ridge sloping off to the west, or other salient characteristic), make note of any intersecting roads, and notable signs or markers. Once you're in your target area, but still on your main route, note your mileage. It's critical to know exactly how far you traveled from Point A, to the point where you're going to turn off the main road and scout out some locations. Copious notes are critical. Your note taking should be so thorough that you could give your notes to someone else, and without a map, they could find your location. My suggestion is that you want to find a remote area off the main road, that is not visible from the road (perhaps a few miles off the road), where you will not be observed, is on public land and you have a right to be there, and where the terrain varies. You don't want to bury your cache on a ridge, as ridgelines can change, they are more likely traveled by humans and animals, and typically the ground (for digging) on a ridge is harder (evidenced by its resistance to erosion). Likewise, you don't want to bury your cache in a ravine, wash, arroyo, or canyon. These are subject to erosion by water flow, and human and animal travel, as well. Midway up, between a low ridge and a wash or stream bed, is probably the best place. Again, with your lensatic compass, take bearings from geographic points to your exact cache site, and note them on your topographic maps. You can take GPS coordinates as well, but remember you may not be able to rely on the GPS unit itself. Note the magnetic bearing from where you parked your car and pace off the distance, heading on that magnetic reading, to the cache site. Note where you parked your car by taking bearings off geographic points. Again, make copious notes. Don't rely on foliage, trees, or sign posts at this point. They die, get cut down, or removed. I cannot tell you how many times I've returned to dig up a cache, and the area was not as I remembered it at all. I spent nearly an entire day searching for one of my cache sites because my notes were sloppy, and the course of the arroyo had changed with a flashflood or two. How I ended up finding it was by triangulating the magnetic bearings I had taken on salient rock outcroppings, and a rocky hill, pinpointing the intersection of bearing lines on the topo, and then digging. There just under the surface, was the reflective engineering tape that I tie to my cache so I know I'm over it.

Burying the cache is basically an exercise in digging. I typically bury three 5 gallon (plastic) containers of gasoline, one 5 gallon (plastic) carboy of water, and plastic storage box with some high calorie ration bars. I camouflage my containers by painting them with camouflage patterns (very easy to do; take 4 colors: beige, brown, light green, and dark green and with a brush, dab with "hit strokes" the colors at random about the container). You can, of course, add any other supplies you want. The hole I dig is something like 3' X 4' X 3' deep. Depending upon the ground, it can be done in a few minutes, or it can take an hour or more (while a folding shovel is usually part of a B.O.B., when heading out to cache, I always take along a full size shovel and small pickaxe; they make the work easier). I don't line the hole with anything (lined holes don't drain well); I simply drop the containers into the hole, tie a 3' piece of 1" wide reflective engineer tape to one of the container handles, string it toward the edge of the hole so it will be covered up just barely under the surface and then with my shovel, I cover up the hole with about 18" of dirt, and pack it down. I use the Lone Ranger and Tonto method of covering my excavation. I brush over it, kick loose dirt around, throw some rocks over it, and stand back to see if it looks "natural". It usually does. I then "sweep" away my footprints as best I can. If the containers should be exposed by whatever, the camouflaging of the containers will help maintain their concealment. Back at the car, I double check my bearings and notes, and then head out. Cache (Point B) done!

I will add here, I referenced parking the vehicle and walking to your cache site (it doesn't have to be far; perhaps only 50' or 100' off your road or track will suffice). I do this for several reasons. One, tire tracks don't go away as easily as footprints. Many times, I have followed tire tracks just to see where they go. Other people do this too. If I see tracks that head up to "nowhere" and they stop and turn around, or go no further, I wonder why they went there; it sparks a curiosity in me. And the same curiosity in someone else may lead that someone to discovering your cache. If you bury your cache with a piece of red engineer tape just under the dirt (as I do), it can be exposed by rain or wind. Second, If you drive up to within a 100' of your cache site, make sure you have your distances and compass bearings, as you would have if you counted your paces from a parked vehicle. Many times over the years, I have returned to the same places in the desert or wilderness, and it never ceases to amaze me how different the places look to me each time; almost never just as I had remembered them. If you drove close to your cache site, after you've buried your cache, don't just turn around and head back over the same tracks you came in on. Continue forward (if you can) and make a loop back to the dirt road. If you can't make a loop, continue your drive forward another few hundred yards, and then turn around. By doing this, you disguise the reason for the diversion to your cache site, suggesting to anyone who might follow your tracks you just made a loop or went on further; nothing more. Another strategy I have used, is to bury my cache near many tire tracks. With many tracks going here and going there, no one set of tracks attracts attention. Be clever!

Your next cache (presumably Point C) is done exactly the same way. Make sure you keep good records and notes on odometer readings. If off road, make note of compass bearings and the mileage you travel at a bearing, and of course, note your travel on your topographical maps.

If you're hiking (or bicycling), caching is done exactly the same way.

EMP's and Protecting Electronic Devices

Electronic devices are conveniences we have come to take for granted. In the event of an EMP, the electromagnetic pulse emitted (either by coronal solar mass ejection of electro-static particles, or by gamma ray electro-magnetic pulse generated by detonation of a high altitude nuclear device) will fry micro-circuitry. In 1859, and again in 1921, solar mass ejections were so powerful, they nearly took down all telegraph operations around the world. Telegraph is not very high tech and involves no micro-circuitry, yet wires burned and power sources blacked out. The rails of train track routes received so much electro-magnetic energy, the steel tracks literally ignited the wooden ties on fire. Today, our electronic devices rely on tiny micro circuits that operate on micro-volts and are subject to burnout in the event of an EMP. Our power grids are reliant upon transformers and switches and computer controls that will burn out in the event of an EMP. In cutting to the chase here, experts and scientist agree, a strong EMP will shut down everything electronic. Not only will production equipment, transportation logistics, distribution, stores, banks, telephones, radios, computers, lights, water and gas service all shut down, everything we rely on today, will go black, and it will be months, if not years before the electricity comes back on again. Why? Because the United States has not invested in hardening our electric grids and replacement switches and transformers are not made in the U.S. and would prove impossible to obtain, even within months or years. An EMP will fry, unless protected, everything we rely on, including flashlights, batteries, portable radios, two-way radios, generators, electric motors, cars, trucks, and the list goes on ad infinitum. If it is electrical, electronic, or has any circuitry at all, it is subject to burn out. Fortunately, humans and animals are not affected in any way, and will feel nothing. The only way we'll know an EMP has struck, is when the power goes down and doesn't come back up, and our electronic conveniences quit.

Our power went out recently, and the first thing I did was look at my wristwatch to see if it was still running. My wristwatch is typical of those worn by most people. It's battery operated and has a small micro-circuit. If the outage had been caused by and EMP, my watch would have stopped.

So how do we get some of our electronic essentials to survive an EMP? We can use a device called a Faraday Cage. It, effectively, is a shield that blocks the electro-magnetic energy from reaching the electronic circuits we need to protect and reroutes the energy to the ground. An EMP is not like a lightning strike. I think it would be fair to compare lightning to a stream of water versus an EMP to a heavy, all encompassing mist. With lightning, the energy must find a single path to the ground. With an EMP, the energy permeates everything, and burns out anything conductive that is sensitive to high voltage.

A Faraday Cage can be a metal mesh around a frame or it can be a simple metal container, like a galvanized trash can (with an insulating bottom under your electronic devices inside the container). The theory is that the electro-magnetic energy is received as static. A Faraday Cage collects the energy as static and then discharges it to the ground or into the ambient atmosphere; the energy/static is directed around the circuitry contained within the cage. The larger the cage, the more static it collects, the more static it collects, the more the energy must be directly routed to a ground. Smaller containers (up to about the size of a trash can, can disperse static merely by being in contact with the ground or into the atmosphere, if the humidity is such that it is conductive). Larger Faraday Cages need to be grounded directly. There are plenty of books addressing Faraday Cages; get one and read up on EMP's and Faraday Cages. I mention them here because your essential electronics need to be protected.

Items to store in a Faraday Cage:

- two way radios
- emergency AM-FM radio
- solar chargers
- rechargeable batteries
- laptops
- flashlights
- laser pointers
- lanterns (battery operated)
- calculators
- digital cameras

- ☐ watches (most wrist watches today are battery powered and use micro-circuitry)
- ☐ any other electronic devices (the ones you want to have after the catastrophe)
- ☐ tools (battery powered)
- ☐ motor vehicle (If newer than 1984, it's most likely controlled by a computer and while you can't practically put your vehicle in a Faraday Cage, you can ground it by a light chain screwed to the frame, that touches the ground)

Planning for Long Term Survival

So... planning and proper preparation isn't so simple, is it? Long term survival preparation adds layer upon layer of additional dimensions to your planning and preparation. I'll just mention some of the planning considerations here, but this book is not a complete encyclopedia of "How-To's". My intention here is to open eyes. Lots of eyes are already opening with mini-series like "Doomsday Preppers" on the National Geographic Channel and radio talk shows like Coast to Coast AM. But, we're still very much in the awakening period and millions upon millions of people all across America and the world have no clue whatsoever what a Bug Out Bag is, or why anyone would even think about having to survive a coming catastrophe. What catastrophe? Right?

Long term survival means surviving after the catastrophe and its consequences upon life as we have known it. Essentially, it means being self-sufficient or co-dependent within a tribe or community (but not in the sense of the word used in pop-psychology terminology).

To some, self-sufficiency is an adventurous concept; almost romantic in a sense. I have heard of, and I know personally, some people who have spent tens, if not hundreds, of thousands of dollars preparing for survival for themselves and families. They have fortified their homes and stocked up on a year or more supplies. Or, they have an outpost somewhere in a remote, rural location. They have turned it into a fortress surrounding their property with concertina wire or razor tape, motion detector alarms, trip wires, and booby traps. The citadel is off-grid with solar and wind turbine power generation with battery backup. The water supply comes from a year round source such as a river, a stream, a spring, or a well and is pumped to an elevated holding tank or cistern through means of Aero Motors (windmills), hydraulic rams, electric pumps, or hand pumps, where gravity flow supplies the household and crop fields. Some of these long-term preppers have brood stock from aquatic ecosystems raising fish to pastures and pens raising rabbits, goats, sheep, chickens, cows, cattle, and horses. They have orchards and are growing everything from citrus fruits, to avocados, to nuts, to apples and cherries. The gardens grow every table vegetable found at most markets or produce stores. And members of the family or tribe have or are becoming proficient farmers, ranchers, gardeners, hunters, butchers, canners, mechanics, carpenters, plumbers, and electricians. Some of these fortresses have machine shops, small lumber mills, carpenter shops, armories, and huge food cellars. I know of one that has a dedicated field to growing sugar beets to use in the alcohol distilling process for producing the ethanol to power the truck, jeep, quad, and tractor that have been converted to burn pure ethanol. They have stocked up on virtually everything one could think of to never have to leave the compound. They have a supply of steel, lumber, pipe, plastics, fabrics, screen and cage wire, nails, bolts, screws, solvents, glues, tools and a list of hardware items that would make Home Depot proud. I know a few who have spent a million dollars or more preparing to survive for years or decades. With enough money, there is no end to the degree one could go to assure complete self-sufficiency. However, I believe it can become an obsession too.

The history of our own old west frontier might be the best place to look to see how people managed to live without the modern day conveniences we are planning to have to live without. Single families with two, three, or four members living in the wild were not as successful as those living within communities (or tribes, if you will). Communities a hundred and fifty years ago were groups of large extended families where roles and responsibilities were defined and work was shared and performed accordingly. The sharing of work meant more things got done, and were done more proficiently as some members acquired skill sets through specialization; specialization that became a valuable asset to the community; as in "butcher, baker, and candlestick maker".

Communities did more than spread the work load around. The members served as mitigators of conflict, moderators of communication, and a force of social persuasion. They brought cooperative civility to an otherwise renegade establishment. I would be a hard person to convince that the lone families who have established isolated fortresses, no matter how sophisticated, are going to fare as well as those who come together in a community environment. And this is where I will assert that in preparation for long term survival, the inclusion of a community of like-minded people is essential. Not only is the professional and trade talent more diverse in a community, the support network for social creatures, as we are, lends itself to psychological success, for the attainment of the common goal of survival. Simply put, the band of brothers will always be more successful at achieving its goal than the lone soldiers fighting individual wars.

Some survival preppers are buying "time shares" (if you will) in multi-million dollar bunker systems. The bunker systems I'm aware of are high tech, modern day, architecturally engineered, and fully self-contained marvels. A bunk, a locker, and a chair in the mess hall can cost several hundred thousand dollars, and while they may be a safe haven, you probably will have never met the gad fly you have to sit down next to, to eat your first MRE. I can imagine the social tensions and conflicts that will arise in these underground prisons, when personality differences erupt into the dramas portrayed on Survivor, the game show. I'm not convinced, in the event of the catastrophe, you could get out to that remote desert location before the "lock down" anyway.

In my opinion, the isolationist in the wilderness fortress and the millionaire bunker buddies are not going to find surviving long term all what they think it will be. The real survivors, at least the successful survivors are going to be the preppers who prepare with a community, or at least with intentions of being part of a community. Their end results will most certainly be more socially and psychologically satisfying, and certainly less stressful and, no doubt, a lot less expensive than those who try to go it alone, or those who buy into a pre-packaged "time share".

A long term survival prep "checklist" (below) outlines some of the items, supplies, and systems that might be considered for long term survival. Depending on what "long term" means, it may be too extensive, adequate, or inadequate. No one can know the future and thus making up such a checklist is, again, just an idea generator. If you are going to become a prepper, or already have become one, I would hope that you realize the benefits of the community approach. One, the community approach defrays cost because redundancy of supplies can be avoided. Two, specialized equipment (for example; HAM radio gear, welding equipment, more technical medical equipment) may very well require that one person, found within the community, who is more skilled using it, or fixing it. Three, that a community with a clear likelihood of having more items, in more diversity, with more members specialized to do it, make it, or fix it, is one more capable of responding to its needs and the needs of its members.

Without political commentary intended, I refer to Randy Weaver and the Ruby Ridge Incident. Here was a man, with a family, who had created an outpost that was approaching nearly complete self-sufficiency. He had the power system, the lookouts, the alarms, the garden, the water, and all the guns he could possibly need. I am

117

quite sure, before his fateful day, he figured he could ride out or defeat any adversary, manmade or delivered by mother nature. When the federal agents arrived and the shooting began, many unfortunate things happened, but perhaps the most unfortunate was that Randy Weaver didn't anticipate the worst case scenario, there was no "community", other than his family, and when the family was shot up, there was nobody to help anybody. Barring a warlike conflict, involving many, many troops, that would not happen in a "civilized" democratic community. I know the first thought that comes to mind when I say that, but Koresh's compound in Waco was centered around a somewhat eclectic ideology. I'm not criticizing Koresh's ideology; I am saying that the purpose of Koresh's community was primarily to promote, among its members, a theology and it was done under a theocracy (of sorts), not as a democracy for the "survival" of the community. In the case of the Waco incident, survival could have been achieved; the community (collectively and democratically), not David Koresh, could have decided what was in their best interest.

A similar and yet more tragic example is the Bobby Jones commune in Guiana.

Unless the catastrophic event is invasion by an overwhelming military force, resulting in annihilation of people, or a formidable martial force imposing a socio-political agenda (e.g., mid-thirties Nazi Germany and the Jewish population), then being a member of a community with a democratic structure, is the system most likely to result in your "long term" survival success.

The long term survival equipment to be acquired should be tuned to the arts and skills (identified) of those persons within the community and hopefully the acquisition of the following items is a community project. With the sharing of expenses and storage logistics, much more can be accomplished. Since I can't know the size of your "community" (whether a family, extended family, or larger community), the quantities of the listed items will have to be determined by you or by consensus. There are numerous books on "how much" to have for 6 months, 1 year, etc. In the Food Category (and some others), I will try to indicate amounts I believe to be sufficient for 1 person, for 1 year. Multiply these quantities by the number of people in your "community". Keep in mind this is just an estimate and children and older adults may not require as much; a 250 lb. man is going to require more than a 110 lb. woman. Except for food items, this checklist (below) should be IN ADDITION TO the B.O.B. and Vehicle checklists, unless items are unnecessarily redundant. Many items need not be redundant.

A. Water

    ☐ Indentified, adequate source for number of people for long term requirements (minimum 1 gallon per person per day)

    ☐ Purification methods in order of best to adequate:
- o distilling
- o filtering and boiling (boil 8 minutes at sea level)
- o bleach or pool shock

- ☐ High volume ceramic water Filter or other filtering device(s) capable of delivering 1 gallon per day per person
- ☐ High volume distiller or multiple stove top distillers capable of distilling 1 gallon per day per person
- ☐ Bleach (regular unscented household) for purifying water (3 drops per quart, 1/2 teaspoon per 5 gallons; 1/2 gallon per every 2 people per year)
- ☐ Pool Shock (commercial chlorinator for purifying water; 1 level tablespoon per 5 gallons)

B. Shelter

- ☐ home(s), outpost, ranch, farm
- ☐ if encampment, portable tent(s), RV(s), boat(s)
- ☐ blankets, sleeping bags, cots, pads, tarps (1 ea. per person)

C. Food

(Food list includes ample items for baking; e.g., no one is likely to eat eggs every day. The quantity of powdered eggs and powdered milk includes an estimated quantity that would be required in baking for one person, as well). Since food preservation, once opened may be an issue, I refer to package/can quantities in smaller sizes. One doesn't want to waste a half eaten #10 can of chili, when two 10 oz. cans could have been consumed, leaving no open, unused food. Regarding food storage, I buy my containers at U.S. Plastics (www.usplastic.com) I buy food grade, airtight drums for dry stocks, and USDA approved carboys for water.

- ☐ high shelf life prepared meals (dehydrated, freeze dried, MRE's); varietal (as much as you can or want to afford); 365 meals per person, per year

- canned meats, stews, soups, beans, chili; varietal; 365 X 10 ounce cans per person, per year
- canned vegetables; varietal; 365 X 7 ounces per person, per year (183 - 14 oz. cans)
- canned fruits; varietal; 365 X 7 ounces per person, per year (183 - 14 oz. cans)
- powdered eggs; 730 ounces per person, per year
- powdered milk; 730 ounces per person, per year
- condensed milk; 104 X 10 ounces per person, per year
- dried fruits, nuts, trail mix; 365 X 4 ounces per person, per year
- coffee, tea, hot chocolate, etc. 365 X 3 servings per person, per year (3 per day)
- drink flavorings (crystal lite, kool aid, tang, etc. 365 X 2 servings per day per person)
- Moringa Oleifera Powder 26 lbs. (1/2 lb. per person per week

Note: Moringa is a "whole food", i.e., one could literally subsist on

Moringa and water alone. Please visit www.moringafarms.com

☐ bulk staples (and appropriate airtight storage containers)

- o salt (4 - 26 oz. containers per person per year)
- o baking powder (4 lbs.)
- o baking soda (2 lbs.)
- o sugar (20 lbs. per person per year)
- o white flour (60 lbs. per person per year)
- o corn flour (20 lbs. per person per year)
- o corn starch (15 lbs. per person per year)
- o pastas (24 lbs. per person per year - if inclined, you can make your own pasta from dough)
- o white rice (60 lbs. per person per year; not brown rice... it doesn't have a good shelf life)

- beans (dried); variety; (100 lbs. per person per year)
- grains; wheat, oats, barley, corn, etc., variety; (120 lbs. per person per year)
- vegetable oil (13 gals. per person per year)
- vinegar (4 gals. per person per year)
- spices and spice mixes (52 ozs. per person per year)
- sauces (hot sauces, Teriyaki, Worcestershire, etc.)
- salad dressings (bottled)
- peanut butter (5 lbs.)
- honey (4 lbs.)
- jams, jellies (4 lbs.)
- shortening, canned (10 lbs.)

The following is the list published by The Church of Jesus Christ of Latter-Day Saints (Mormon Church) as the suggested stores for 1 person for 1 month. It does not differ significantly from what I've listed, but I've added it here for your reference:

Grains:
- o wheat   12.5 lbs.
- o flour   2.08 lbs.
- o corn meal   2.08 lbs.
- o oats   2.08 lbs.
- o rice   4.17 lbs.
- o pasta   2.08 lbs.

Fats and Oils:
- o shortening   0.33 lbs.
- o vegetable oil   0.17 gals.
- o mayonnaise   0.17 qts
- o salad dressing   0.08 qts.
- o peanut butter   0.33 lbs.

Legumes
- o beans, dry   2.50 lbs.
- o lima beans   0.42 lbs.
- o soy beans   0.83 lbs.
- o split peas   0.42 lbs.
- o lentils   0.42 lbs.
- o dry soup mix   0.42 lbs.

Sugars
- o honey   0.25 lbs.

- o sugar, gran. white   3.33 lbs.
- o sugar, brown   0.25 lbs.
- o molasses   0.08 lbs.
- o corn syrup   0.25 lbs.
- o jams, jellies   0.25 lbs.
- o fruit drink powder   0.50 lbs.
- o flavored gelatin   0.08 lbs.

Milk
- o dry milk   5.00 lbs.
- o evaporated milk   1.00 can
- o other   1.08 lbs.

Cooking Essentials
- o baking powder   0.08 lbs.
- o baking soda   0.08 lbs.
- o yeast   0.04 lbs.
- o salt   0.42 lbs.
- o vinegar   0.04 gals.

Water
- o water   30.50 gals.
- o bleach   0.08 gals.

- ☐ recipes
  - o instructions on canning; hot water and steaming
  - o breads

- o tortillas
- o biscuits and rolls
- o cakes
- o puddings
- o meat dishes
- o vegetable dishes
- o pasta dishes
- o bean dishes
- o rice dishes

D. Cooking, Housekeeping, and Food Prep

- ☐ Cooking equipment
  - o camp stove (<u>more than one is a must</u>, using a variety of fuels from wood, to fuel pellets, to Coleman fuel, unleaded gasoline, propane)
  - o cast iron wood stove
  - o Coleman fuel (15 gals. per person per year)
  - o unleaded gasoline (if dual fuel stove, substitute for Coleman fuel)
  - o propane (as needed for 2 hour burn time per day)

- fuel pellets (depending on stove, figure 2 hour burn X 365)
- fire wood
- camp oven
- camp grill
- griddle
- waterproof matches (boxes "strike anywhere"; min. 120 boxes @ 50 ea.)
- magnesium-steel strike matches
- lighters (Bic, and long reach)
- BBQ (select a high quality unit)
- charcoal
- fire starters (pellets, cotton balls doused in Vaseline (petroleum jelly), small 2" cardboard "tents" with wax dripped over, mineral spirits, etc.)
- lighter fluid
- sterno cans

☐ Utensils

- plates (reusable plastic or aluminum)
- cups
- pots
- pans
- skillets
- pressure cooker (lowers cooking time, and preserves nutrients)
- percolator (coffee, hot water); non-electric
- knives
- spatulas
- spoons
- tongs
- forks
- can openers
- cork screw
- common eating utensils (knives, forks, spoons, etc.)

☐ Cast Iron items
- cast iron fire heated old fashion iron (many uses)
- cast iron wood stove (mentioned again; think 150 years ago)
- cast iron cookware

- o Dutch ovens (versatile for myriad items)
- o griddle
- o fry pans
- ☐ Other essential food prep items
  - o hand cranked meat grinder (a "must" if preparing game)
  - o hand cranked grain mill (high quality enough to make fine flour from your grains; this is an "almost" essential item)
  - o hand cranked mincer and pasta maker
  - o scissors (high quality)
  - o knife sharpener
  - o gloves
  - o pot holders
  - o aluminum foil
  - o mason jars (essential)
  - o food storage containers (plastic)
  - o plastic storage bags (quart and gallon size)
  - o fire poker
  - o wire brush
  - o dish wash basin or tub

- o detergent
- o hand and dish towels
- o scrubbing sponges, Brillo Pads
- o Ajax or Bar Keepers

E. Clothing and Personal Items

- ☐ Clothing
  - o underwear
  - o socks
  - o pants
  - o shirts
    NOTE: Clothing is a source of string, thread, and fiber. Clothing is suitable for additional bandages.
  - o belts
  - o jackets
  - o hats
  - o gloves
  - o shoes
  - o boots
  - o rain poncho
- ☐ Personal Items

- combat knife (high quality, stainless steel, full tang
- glasses
- reading glasses (min. 3 pairs)
- sun glasses
- magnifying glass (you can see splinters and stingers with it, and it can start a fire by magnifying and focusing direct sunlight)
- mirror (high polish stainless steel, reflection and signaling)
- laser rescue flare (or other high powered laser)
- cell phone (may or may not work)
- cell phone solar charger
- binoculars, telescope, night scope
- watches
- calculator (solar or battery operated)
- rucksack or backpack

- writing materials (pens and pencils)
- ruler
- drafting triangles
- protector
- tape measure
- notebook
- books (entertainment, survival guides, instruction manuals, repair manuals, etc.)
- maps (topographic and road)
- divider compass
- lensatic sighting compass
- camera (even though digital computer may not be available, camera can still record events)
- towels
- soap
- chair(s)
- _____

F. Medications

☐ Prescriptions

- o whatever you need for 1 year; medications will be extremely difficult to find
- o antibiotics (broad spectrum)
- o antibiotic ointments
- ☐ Over the counter remedies
  - o Iodine tablets
  - o aspirin
  - o ibuprophin (advil, motrin, etc.)
  - o tylinol
  - o decongestants
  - o lotions
  - o vitamins, etc.
  - o sun block lotion, zinc oxide
  - o insect repellent, deet

G. First Aid

- ☐ High quality and complete kit, to include:
  - o bandages (variety strip type)
  - o butterfly bandages

- adhesive tape (narrow to wide and ample length)
- gauzes
- strips of cotton sheet material (2" X 36")
- squares of cotton sheet material (36" X 36")
- self-adhesive ("ace") bandage or wrap
- que tips
- cotton balls
- anti-bacterials (Betadine, iodine, isopropanol alcohol, and peroxide)
- anti-fungal ointment (tolphanate)
- scissors (high quality stainless steel)
- tweezers (high quality stainless steel)
- surgical blade (high quality stainless steel)
- magnifying glass (mentioned already several times - can't stress it enough)
- analgesics, pain killers

- suture kit
- inflatable splints
- first aid instruction manual

H. Lighting, Electricity, and Heating

- ☐ Flashlights (can't have too many)
    - LED type, min. 200 lumens, use only AAA, AA, C, D cells. The NiCad G3, etc. are worthless and not rechargeable without electric power. Solar chargers are available and work great with common US size batteries (NO funky camera batteries)
    - rechargeable batteries
- ☐ Lanterns (Coleman, kerosene and battery powered)
    - appropriate fuel (min. 1 year; 50 gallons)
    - rechargeable batteries (AAA, AA, C, D, 9V)

137

- ☐ Solar panel for recharging batteries (for every battery type - AAA, AA, C, D, 9V)
- ☐ Oil lamps (min. 1 for each room)
  - ○ lamp oil (adequate supply; 50 gals.)
  - ○ replacement wicks
- ☐ Candles
- ☐ Battery bank(s), and regulator
- ☐ Wind turbine
- ☐ Solar charging panels (high wattage for off grid power)
- ☐ Inverter
- ☐ Electric generator (with sufficient fuel)
- ☐ Big Buddy Heater(s) (propane), with minimum of three 20 gal. Propane bottles
- ☐ Portable kerosene heaters

I. Communication Devices

- ☐ Two way radios
  - ○ FRS/GMRS
  - ○ CB
  - ○ VHF, UHF
  - ○ HAM

138

- o rechargeable batteries; use radios that utilize common batteries (AAA, AA, C, D, etc.)
- ☐ AM FM, weather, shortwave radio (battery, solar, crank, or combination of power)

All electronics kept in Faraday cages if possible

J. Self Defense Weapons

- ☐ Firearms
- ☐ Ammunition (appropriate quantities)
- ☐ taser
- ☐ pepper spray
- ☐ gun cleaning kit
- ☐ knives
- ☐ clubs
- ☐ batons
- ☐ hatchets
- ☐ spears
- ☐ bows and arrows
- ☐ crossbows and bolts
- ☐ traps and snares

☐ concertina, barbed wire, razor
ribbon

K. Pets and Animals

Dogs are great comfort as are cats.
Dogs can be great advance warning
systems, provide a degree of security,
and/or defense. Horses and other
animals can do work. While some
may forage or grub, others will need
food.
☐ Food supplies for your pets,
animals, and food stock
animals
☐ Medications or treatments (e.g.
flea, de-
worming treatments) they may
need as well.
☐ Leashes, leads, halters, ropes
☐ Collars, harnesses (reflective)
☐ Identification tags (RFID chips
may be worthless without
power and scanners)

L. Hunting and Fishing for Food

- ☐ Fishing gear; fly and lure, rods reels, and tackle
- ☐ Firearms and other self-defense items serve for hunting as do traps, snares, and pitfalls.

M. Tools
- ☐ Hand tools
  - o combat knife (high quality, full tang, stainless)
  - o knife sharpener or stone
  - o axes
  - o splitting wedges
  - o sledge hammers
  - o saws (buy only high quality)
    - o crosscut log saw (high quality - Western Log Saw)
    - o ripping saw
    - o pruning saw (folding)
    - o coping saw
    - o miter saw
    - o hack saw
  - o saw blades (extra)
  - o framing hammer
  - o ball peen hammer

- rubber mallet
- wooden mallet
- nails (variety)
- screws (variety)
- bolts (variety), with nuts and washers
- cold chisels
- punches
- wood chisels
- pry bars
- shovels
- picks
- adjustable wrenches
- open end and box wrenches
- socket wrenches
- pipe wrenches
- screwdrivers (variety)
- Leatherman all-purpose tool
- vise
- anvil
- forging hammers
- vice grips
- ropes (variety of sizes and strengths, nylon, poly, and manila)
- chain (variety of sizes and weights)
- cable come-along (winch)

- cord (parachute, jute)
- string (rolls nylon, cotton)
- wire (common bailing wire)
- fasteners
- gloves
- spray paint (variety colors)
- paint (buckets or cans) camouflage colors of beige, brown, green, black)
- paint brushes
- putty, fillers, Bondo
- putty knife
- sealants
- jeweler's tools
- files
- sandpaper, abrasive cloth
- drills (brace and bit)
- tap and die sets
- planes
- adze
- rakes
- hoes
- trowels
- shovels
- machete
- broom
- wire cutters
- sheet metal sheers

- o pliers (variety)
- o scissors
- o bolt cutters (large and small)
- o grinder/sharpener (hand cranked if you can find one)
- o tape measure and other measuring and drawing tools
- o utility knives with many extra blades
- o Duct Tape, Duct Tape, and Duct Tape, etc.
- o Acetylene welding equipment with extra Oxy and Acetylene
- o welding rod, brazing rod
- o arc welding equipment
- o welding rod
- o soldering Iron and solder (old fashion fire heated, and electric)
- o solder
- o flux
- o propane brazing torch
- o MAP gas torch kit
- o wire brush

- o generator, if possible with adequate fuel
- o solar charging panels and regulators (can't say enough about getting high wattage solar panels for charging everything from small batteries for radios, flashlights, lanterns, cameras, to E-Bike batteries, to maintaining "off grid" battery banks)
- o battery banks
- o wind Turbine
- o electrical wire (variety gauges)
- o extension cords
- o outlcts
- ☐ If off grid, then:
  - o power tools:
  - o drills
  - o saws, etc
- ☐ Hand cranked water pump (electric also, if off grid power available), min. 1 gal. per min. with 15' draw capacity

☐ Fuel pump (automotive type), 12 volt, with 20' rubber hose (fuel suitable) and hose clamps

☐ Hand (air) Pump, battery powered air compressor (if off grid, electric, also)

☐ Alcohol Still (it makes great fuel for almost anything and cars (with slight modification) CAN run on it (there's a great book - Alcohol Can Be A Gas by Blume, available at Amazon) - (a good still is available from http://www.milehidistilling.com/)

N. Supply Stockpiles

☐ Variety of fabrics:
  o tarps
  o sheets clear plastic
  o sheets black plastic (covers windows well, absorbs heat well - however, it does reflect light; for covering windows, I have a

12'X12' piece of black dense cotton fabric)

- o canvas
- o nylon
- o cotton
- o linen
- o mosquito netting
- o metal screen material
- o nylon screen material
- o sewing needles
- o thread
- o grommet tools
- o seam tape
- o seam glue or adhesive
- Lumber
  - o boards
  - o beams
  - o studs
  - o plywood
  - o osb, particle board, and MDF
- Variety nails and screws
- Rope, Chain, and cable (variety sizes, and weight)
- Variety of steel stock, variety of sizes: bar, flat, angle, solid square, sheet, tube, rebar.

- Variety of cinder block, bricks, cement and mortar mix
- Variety of PVC Pipe, variety of sizes, fittings, and glue
- Variety of copper tubing, fittings, and valves, tube cutter, extra solder
- Asphalt roofing material (rolled, shingles, etc)
- Containers and buckets with and without lids: plastic, wood, metal (variety)
- Hoses; rubber and plastic, tubing, and fittings.
- Glues, adhesives, sealers
- Solvents (denatured alcohol, mineral spirits, paint thinner, lacquer thinner, and acetone)
- Fiberglass cloth, mat, and rope
- Resin and catalyst
- Paper buckets
- Charcoal and hardwood firewood, lighter fluid, fuels appropriate for stoves, heaters, etc.
- Fencing: rolls of chain link, chicken wire, 1/2" X 1/2" cage

wire, hardware cloth, screening, posts, poles, and fasteners
- ☐ Paper Towels (however many rolls you can store)

O. Porta Potty

- ☐ 5 gallon bucket
  - o ample plastic trash bags
  - o "fitting" toilet seat (fits over top of 5 gallon bucket
- ☐ Toilet paper, tissue (min. 80 rolls per person per year)
- ☐ Lime (4 - 50 lb. sacks per person per year; alkalizes waste and reduces odors)
- ☐ Instructions on how to dig a latrine for long term use

P. Bathing

- ☐ Soap
- ☐ Shampoo
- ☐ Towels
- ☐ Wash cloths
- ☐ Washtubs

☐ Propane camp water heater, or, milk can or large pot for heating water or plastic 5 gallon Sun Shower

Q. Transportation

☐ Bicycle with basket (wheels go faster and farther than feet)
☐ Electric powered bike/trike with basket (and solar panel for charging without elec. service). In my opinion an Electric Tricycle with a rear cargo basket would be one of the best investments one could make. With a good 20 Watt solar panel and regulator, the battery of the trike could be charged indefinitely and you would have motorized, transportation with cargo carrying capacity. If you give this thought, the solar regulator used is different for a lead acid battery than another used for a NiCad battery; be sure to get the

correct regulator. You can also consider foam filled tires as opposed to inflated)

- ☐ Dirt Bikes (with fuel and oil)
- ☐ Quads (with fuel and oil)
- ☐ Good, large, heavy duty pull wagon (person pull)
- ☐ Golf Cart or Utility Vehicle (Battery or gasoline with extra fuel)
- ☐ Car (converted to use alcohol as fuel)
- ☐ Truck (converted to use alcohol as fuel)
- ☐ Extra fuel
- ☐ Utility trailer
- ☐ Mechanics tools
- ☐ Tire repair kits
- ☐ Refer to Vehicle Check List

R. Books, manuals, and literature (remember... no Internet. You need to have your sources of information (and entertainment). Build a library. The availability of literature on the subject of survival is extensive. Here are a few I've read and consider informative:

- [ ] SAS Survival Guide (Wiseman; Amazon)
- [ ] The Forager's Harvest (Thayer; Amazon)
- [ ] Survival Guide for the End of the World as We Know It (Rawles; Amazon)
- [ ] The Joy of Cooking (Rombauer and Beckman; Amazon)
- [ ] Dressing and Cooking Wild Game (Marrone; Amazon)
- [ ] Primitive Technology (Westcott; Amazon)
- [ ] Deerskins Into Buckskins (Richards; Amazon)
- [ ] The Rural Ranger, Snares and Traps for Urban and Suburban Survival (Foster; Amazon)
- [ ] How To Trapping (Overton; Amazon)
- [ ] How To Survive Anywhere (Nyerges, Amazon)
- [ ] The Complete Do-It-Yourself Manual (Editors Family Handyman; Amazon)

- ☐ The Vegetable Gardener's Bible (Smith; Amazon)
- ☐ 1801 Home Remedies (Editors Reader's Digest; Amazon)
- ☐ Alcohol Can Be A Gas (Blume; Amazon)

Many authors of survival books have different experiences, different knowledge, and different ideas. While many write on the same subjects, some "hit" some topics, while others "hit" other topics. Personally, I don't think it hurts to have two, maybe three books on any given subject.

Download from the Internet (while you can) instructions for making: candles, soap, recipes. Compile instruction and repair manuals for any equipment you have. Assemble binders full of recipes and instructions and put them into your survival library. My downloaded instructions and recipes fill two fat 3 ring binders.

Here's an example of one of many recipes I downloaded:

Flour Tortillas

Serving Size : 12

Ingredients:

- 4 cups Unbleached all purpose flour
- 2 teaspoons Salt
- 4 teaspoons Baking powder
- 2 tablespoons Vegetable shortening
- 1 1/2 cups Warm water or more if needed

Instructions:

In a large bowl, stir together the flour, salt and baking powder. With a pastry blender, a fork or your hands, gradually work in the lard or shortening until it is all incorporated. Add enough warm water to make a soft but not sticky dough. Turn out onto a lightly floured board and knead for 5 minutes. Divide the dough into 1/4 cup (3 oz) portions and form them into balls. Roll each ball into a flat round about 6 inches in diameter and 1/8 inches thick.

Heat a large heavy skillet over medium high heat. Place the tortillas one at a time into the dry hot skillet; cook until brown on one side, then turn and brown the other side. Remove from the skillet and keep warm in cloth towel. Source: Southwest cookbook

Note: Cooking Oil can be used in place of lard or shortening.

- ☐ Notebooks (blank) for keeping notes and sketches
- ☐ Drawing tools: triangles, compass, ruler, straight-line, pencils, erasers, etc.

S. Gardens and crop raising (Seeds)

- ☐ Seeds; variety of non-hybrid, non-GMO vegetable seeds. Give serious consideration to this category. You cannot have enough of these (survival packs with large varieties are available at Amazon). Seeds that are non-hybrid and non-GMO grow crops that produce harvestable seeds capable of germination; keeping you in perpetual supply).

T. Barter Items (you must have barter items. Currency may be worthless)

☐ Cartons Cigarettes
☐ Cases 1/2 pints, or small bottles of Vodka or other liquor
☐ Cases chocolate bars, nutrition bars, ration bars
☐ Coffee and sugar, hot chocolate, powdered drink mixes
☐ Extra boxes matches, lighters
☐ Magnifying glasses (to see with, to start fires with)
☐ Pocket knives
☐ Cheap .22 Cal. Revolvers with 200 rounds .22 Cal.

ammunition to go with each.

☐ Ammunition (boxes of most popular calibers; e.g., .22 long rifle, .223, .38, .357, 9mm, .380, 20 ga., 12 ga., etc.)

☐ Small cans pepper spray (O.C.)

☐ Extra pairs gloves

☐ Small denomination silver coins (pre 1965); dimes and quarters. (at the time of this writing, "junk silver" was worth 22 X face value. One dime was worth $2.20!)

☐ Seed packets (non-hybrid, non-GMO garden vegetables)

☐ Information (verbal and written)

Surviving It

Ideally, your "community" or "tribe" would be based at a rural outpost or ranch(s) with a year round source of water, where you'd have barns, sheds, or even a bunker(s) with shelf after shelf of all the survival supplies and stockpiles you could ever need (cached about your community, of course - "never put all your eggs in one basket"). You could grow crops, raise goats, sheep, rabbits, chickens, hunt and fish. You'd be isolated enough to be out of the reach of the marauding urbanites. Your community would include like minded, multi-talented people with whom you would share your resources, talents, and work. You would have "action plans" already in place, resources identified, and defensive strategies (Plan A, Plan B, Plan C, etc.) already developed. Your community might include skilled persons, tradesmen, and professionals. With a plan and a diverse array of talent, your community might include:

☐ Team Captain

- ☐ Strategy and "think tank" members (creative, intuitive, and well read)
- ☐ Physician (General surgeon)
- ☐ Nurse (Registered, Physician Assistant, or Nurse Practitioner with ER experience)
- ☐ Veterinarian
- ☐ Architect and Civil Engineer
- ☐ Psychologist
- ☐ Electrician (master)
- ☐ Plumber (master)
- ☐ Carpenter (master)
- ☐ Radio Technician and Ham operator
- ☐ IT Tech
- ☐ Blacksmith (and welder)
- ☐ Cook (with good knowledge of basic recipes)
- ☐ Mechanic (auto electric and diesel and gasoline engines)
- ☐ Machinist
- ☐ Hunter (seasoned with extensive game and fowl hunting experience and extensive knowledge of game preparation and preserving)
- ☐ Butcher

- Gardener or Farmer (with extensive knowledge of raising vegetables and crops and small food game)
- Gunsmith
- Trainer in Martial Arts and Self-Defense and combat techniques (Police or military experience)
- Spiritual leader (non-denominational)
- Inter-disciplinary "Jack of All Trades" and "Student" and Instructor of trades and disciplines to others.
- Teacher (classroom general education for families of members)
- 4 to 6 general laborers (intelligent and in good physical condition)
- 6 to 8 "Soldiers" (with active duty experience)
- Survival Specialist (with extensive military training) for our instruction, and as squad leader for "soldiers"
- And lastly, a "constitution" of sorts to establish your social/political structure.

That would be ideal, but not every community can or will reach that level of independence. Were we to achieve this, and were it not for the absence of electricity, fuels, pharmaceuticals, unlimited foods and commodities, we probably would be stepping out of survival mode and into living again. But since this level of sophistication isn't reachable by most of us, nor probably is having every item on these checklists, just having the basics will help us make it.

Don't wait. Do it now. If you haven't PREPARED, when the big one comes, it will be too late.

Summary

There is much, much more that can be said. But since this is a brief plea of persuasion and guide of suggestions, shared anecdotes and precautions, and reference checklists, not a survival encyclopedia, I'm just going to add some comments here.

The checklists in this booklet arise out of having been asked by a few individuals, who are familiar with my experience, to put together a B.O.B. for them, and for a few others who were interested in long term survival (as well as short term), to list the items they can go and buy themselves. I have researched some items and the conclusion I have come to is 1.) quality is necessary, 2.) but for limited use or short term needs, expense should be a consideration. For my friends who asked me to put together a B.O.B., I weighed the quality of an item against the cost to obtain reasonable quality and usually ended up not buying the "Rolls Royce", but the high end "Ford". An example of this is the Ka-Bar Combat Knife versus the M-Tech Combat Knife and the Winchester Bowie Knife (by

Gerber). The Ka-Bar is clearly superior in quality, but it's almost 3 times as expensive, too, and the M-Tech and Winchester knives are of sufficient quality. Given the difference in price, and the fact that the B.O.B. I was putting together was designed for a one week outing, I chose the M-Tech knife. The B.O.B. I ended up putting together for them came in around the $600.00 mark. Since, at first, I thought this was high, I checked other survival outfits to see where there pricing ran. I found the prices to be all over the board, from $39.95 to over $1,300.00. The 39.95 bag, of course, was full of silly, cheap trinkets and gadgets that, however cute and compact, I wouldn't want to have to rely upon the items in it. The $1,300.00 B.O.B. was way over the top on what would be needed to survive in the wilderness for a week or so; I even felt $600 was too much. I explained how and why I selected the items I did, and then when I told my friends what the cost would be (less than the original $600 figure), they didn't blink an eye. They had already shopped the market and found the price I needed to cover the items in the B.O.B. more than reasonable, and considerably less than other B.O.B.'s to which it was clear, had been given less thought. And, it appeared to me as well, with some of the (more expensive) B.O.B.'s I looked into, no real thought was given to what was included as far as quality or reliability goes. Perhaps these outfitters were cutting cost corners to maximize profit, or perhaps the individuals compiling the gear had no experience with it.

An example, one B.O.B. selling for around $750, had a camp cable saw included (sometimes called a hand chain saw) and it was its only saw. They are compact and lightweight, but if you have ever taken one of these along on an outing or camping trip, you know how worthless most of them are. They're awkward to use, they dull very quickly, and for what they are, they're fairly expensive. For a while I used a folding aluminum, backpacking bow saw. It was quite cleverly designed in that the blade folded into the tension arm, which slid inside the handle for compactness. But, I found it to lack dimensional stability and thus the blade frequently flexed and bound up. The best saw I've decided is a simple folding pruning saw. They're inexpensive, available at any hardware store, the blade folds into the handle for compactness, the blade is thicker and thus there is no flex and binding, and they are sharper and remain sharp longer than the other saws.

Everything I've listed (on both, the B.O.B. list, and the long term survival list), I either own, have experience with, or have researched extensively, and I can say with a reasonable degree of confidence, if the items are used properly and cared for properly, they will work for the use(s) intended. Now sure, it wouldn't be fair to say we haven't included some rather "inexpensive" items, along with some very top notch and expensive gear. But, these "inexpensive" items are not intended to serve a lifetime; only a short period of time. Some of them are just "Get-Bys". Maybe I was overly critical of the B.O.B. with the cable saw, but I don't consider the saw (the only one in the bag), to be a "Get-By" item.

When I was a bit younger, just out of college, and very much into the "wilderness and homestead" experience, I had a book called the "Whole Earth Catalog". Perhaps some of you remember it. It was amazing. It was a rather large catalog of "off the grid" items (if you will), and where to buy them. It listed things like hand turned washing machines, umbrella-folding clothes drying lines (try to find one now!), small (but well built) wood burning forge with a hand turned bellows, blacksmith's anvils, solar food dehydrators, Kelty backpacks (the elite of the time), oil lamps, and two-man timber saws. The Whole Earth Catalog was packed with interesting goodies that are not easily found today (except in third world countries), and it was way before the computer and search engines. Today, I would guess Amazon comes about as close as anything to being the best marketplace to find almost anything. I use Amazon extensively, but frequently even Amazon doesn't have what I'm looking for.

In that we could very well find ourselves without power, and very likely, eventually out of the conventional liquid fuels (gasoline, diesel, kerosene, lamp oil, propane, etc.) that we've stockpiled and stored, I tend to think in terms of "hand operated, leg powered", rechargeable (via solar panels) battery driven, or "by-gone-era energy driven" (steam, ethanol, wind, hydraulic, or animal powered) systems (off grid battery systems, the PV solar panel and wind driven turbine generators are modern-day exceptions). The way I think, or "My thought process" ought to be evident by now. I'm not an engineering genius, but I do think a bit outside the box, and I try to anticipate "everything" (albeit, that can be elusive). Alcohol (ethanol) is a fuel that is relatively easy to make (think "moonshiners"). Most people don't know, Henry Ford made his early cars to be dual fueled; i.e., they could burn gasoline or ethanol. Why did he make them this way? Because when the motorist of the early 20th Century left the urban areas where gasoline was available, and drove into the country, the only fuel source was often the farmer with his moonshine still, producing ethanol. Why, in these times of threatened or purported oil shortages and rising fuel costs, America hasn't invested heavily in national large scale production of ethanol for its primary fuel, I don't know. I would only have to guess because there are economic forces, influencing political powers to keep oil/petro fuels (gasoline, diesel, and kerosene) our only main source of energy. I heard arguments that large scale production of ethanol would severely reduce corn and grain supplies needed for food and animal feed. I say B.S. to that. It's misinformation and propaganda to keep Big Oil on top, with their hands in our pockets. We could be completely replacing petro fuels with ethanol, without touching the corn production for food or feed. The sugar beet (especially the fodder beet) will grow just about anywhere in the United States, including arid regions, and it contains 3 times the sugar that corn contains, lending itself to about 3 times the alcohol yield that corn does, and the mash, when the wort is drained off, is one of the best natural fertilizers known, and an excellent animal feed because the fermentation process breaks down the cellulose, making the mash more digestible. Ethanol burns clean (no hydrocarbon emissions), it has a higher octane than gasoline, it is not as dangerous to transport, it's cheaper (by more than two thirds) to produce, and with virtually no significant alteration to engine technology; it can be utilized in any combustion engine, can be used in lieu of home heating oil, and is a wonderful fuel for anything from boilers (electric generation) to stoves.

It's criminal, I believe, that the Big Oil Companies and their political puppets, continue to hold the American people hostage to oil. I heard one political clown, in a rather high position, say the logistics of transporting of ethanol from the Midwest's corn belt to other parts of the country made ethanol distribution unfeasible. What? We pay exorbitant prices to ship oil half way around the planet, in supertankers that rip open and pollute the marine ecosystems for decades, or we sit and watch offshore oil platforms blow up and pollute the gulf for centuries to come. We send some $5 Trillion dollars a year out of our economy into the economies of our enemies, and this guy (and the rest of his special interest political machine) tells us ethanol distribution is not feasible? Hogwash! OK then, how about localized production? Sugar beets grow anywhere; we should adopt the "micro brewery" approach to production, so long distance transportation or piping isn't an argument. Grow the beets locally, distill the ethanol locally, and sell it locally. When are we, as a people, going to wake up take our country back?

I could change my direction in this book to express my rage at the way we're being led around by the nose, for the financial gain of a few. The massive economic force(s) of Big Corporations, Banks, Wall Street, and the FED is directing the political paradigms to make policy based upon their financial interests; not in the interest of the American people, per se. If the government would cut the "fat" out of its behemoth, unwieldy, and grossly inefficient bureaucracy, get out of the stupid and invasive wars, eliminate the pork-barrel political favors, and stop the billions in foreign aid we cast to the wind, it could back off on the taxes and downsize itself out of our faces, and we could get back to work. And if monopolistic and oligarchic corporations were not allowed to "kill" competition through political avenues, people would have more money to spend and the economy would be a whole lot healthier.

We should be outraged that the Big Chemical companies are forcing upon agriculture, genetically engineered organisms (GMO's) in the form of grain crop, and vegetable seeds that don't reproduce and thus force us to buy THEIR seeds, because "they" are gaining control of all seed stock, or they sue the small farmer into oblivion because the non-hybrid, non-GMO seeds blew into their Big Farm Coop Fields. One BIG Chemical company has seen to it that 90% of the sugar beets are now GMO's. What's that about? Could it be that they know something we don't? Maybe large scale ethanol production is on the horizon, after all. Interesting thought, huh? It wouldn't be because they want to control the raw resources for our "new" energy, would it?

The Big Pharmaceutical Companies are lobbying the FDA to force small food supplement, vitamin, and holistic nutrient producers and marketers to engage in prohibitively expensive testing and trials, and await "new" FDA approval, in order to sell their products, when these products have been selling with no harm for decades.

Big Oil, which with Wall Street, effectively controls Washington, keeps us from becoming energy independent, all the while selling U.S. oil overseas where the profits are higher and driving up the cost of oil here for the benefit of their own quarterly returns.

My last comment is about the FED. Here we have a private corporation, whose stock is privately held by a select few, who "create" money at will, out of thin air, lend it to our Treasury, which in turn pays interest on the fiat money produced, which it collects, in the form of taxes, from the American people. What a scam! Who really gets rich off of American productivity? The stockholders of the Federal Reserve Bank. Its sick! THIS is why we need to prepare to survive; because this "private system" of fractional central banking has bankrupted America! And our economy is collapsing, and one way or another, by natural disaster, or by crafted manmade disaster, hyperinflation will result.

But, back to survival gear... I will soon (if I don't already by the time you read this) have a website up (http://www.survivedoom.com) where some of the gear I think is good can be ordered.

I think a water distiller is very good to have for purifying contaminated water. There are some stove top distillers available and I think they're quite good, but they are quite expensive. Distilling water is really quite simple to do, requiring a pretty simple mechanism/apparatus. So I set about to design and make an inexpensive stove top distiller. I wanted to make it using common, everyday, items you can get almost anywhere. I came up with one that is very inexpensive (by comparison), it works adequately well, and can be made by almost anyone, using simple, ordinary materials. On the website (when it's up) I hope to add some photos of what I came up with, with a materials list so you can make one. The cost is comparatively low for all the parts. (http://www.survivedoom.com).

Even thought my distiller didn't end up being made with paint cans, I realized you can do a lot of pretty cool things with an empty (clean and new, unlined) paint cans. While there are some already on the Internet (and some are quite sophisticated), I designed my own wood burning cook stove that uses debris, wood scraps, and sticks, etc. to burn. No special fuels are required. It's a great little emergency cook stove and it gets hot enough cook your meals or boil the water in your homemade distiller to purify your contaminated water. You can make one, and there are numerous examples on the Web on how to make them.

Here's another idea for you. One gallon, new (lined or unlined) paint cans make great Faraday Cages for small electronic items. Cut a 5" diameter circle out of a piece of wood or plywood (3/4" thick). Cut a rectangle out of corrugated cardboard measuring 7" high X 15 3/4" wide. Staple or tack the card board, along the long edge, around the circle of wood, creating a tube 7" high. The bottom of the tube then becomes closed off (with the wood circle). It insulates your electronic items from the bare metal at the bottom of the can, and the cardboard tube (sleeve) insulates your electronic items from the bare metal sides of the can. Then cut two 5 1/2" circles out of cardboard. Place your electronic items inside the tube and tape (using electrician's tape) your double layer cardboard circles on top to seal off the top end of the tube. If you don't want to go to trouble of making the cardboard tube, a half gallon plastic milk container, cut down to (about 6" tall) to fit inside the paint can works fine) Drop your "package" (tube with its electronic contents) into the can, space your tube in the center of the can, put some wadded up paper between the wall of the can and your cardboard (or plastic) tube, put a non-conductive top on your tube and place the metal lid on tightly. You now have your small electronic items protected from an EMP, in a small Faraday Cage. It is small enough where it does not need to be grounded. Pretty simple, huh? This same concept can be applied to any metal container where the top is in good metal to metal contact with the body of the container and your electronic contents are insulated from the metal (ammo cans work too). I believe you can go as large as a 30 gal. galvanized trash can, before it would need to be grounded.

We (my friends and I) have put together a very good and reasonably priced Bug Out Bags (B.O.B.), BOB System, and are making them available to you at a fair price. We've assembled items that we believe are necessary, and we've selected items of high quality, but within reason price-wise. It's a long ways from the $39.95 bag, but it's considerably less than the $1,300 bag, too. You can find it at (http://www.survivedoom.com).

When designing our B.O.B.'s, we decided a "system" of bags was better than one bag. We came up with the (now service marked and copyrighted) concept of the BOB SYSTEM, with BOB ONE, and BOB TWO that complement one another. BOB ONE is the 7 day pack. Add BOB TWO and you have enough gear for 30 days or longer. The system eliminates unnecessary redundancy in equipment, extends quantities of exhaustible gear and supplies, and adds other supplies and gear we thought necessary for extended periods of time.

Also, on our website, we hope to feature some very interesting items that might be very handy when the power goes out and there's no more gasoline to power your conventional generator, and when you need to charge your batteries, to run your water pump, to run your tools, etc.

We are trying to avoid being just another survival products website. There are already plenty of those in cyberspace. We aren't going to compete with the bulk food guys, the Emergency ration guys, the MRE sellers, the camping gear guys, or the emergency radio man. We are, either going to just give you our opinion and tell you what to buy and where to buy it (perhaps providing links to other websites) or if not easily found, or outside-of-the-box, we might offer it for sale.

All of our gear will be of sufficient quality and known, used by us, or thoroughly researched where we can confidently recommend it.

WWW.SURVIVEDOOM.COM will feature a blog where experts, preppers, and practitioners will editorialize on catastrophic scenarios, survival techniques, personal experiences, theoretical situations, supplies, gear, where to find it, and other topics of interest to getting prepared.

I could go on and on with my sharing of experiences (and their inherent lessons), survival gear recommendations, the reason(s) we need to get prepared now, and survival preparedness itself. Since the topic is virtually endless and discussion(s) could (and do) go on and on, We would welcome your emails and comments, where you can tell me I'm nuts, I don't know what I'm talking about, you have had similar experiences, or have recommendations of your own. You can email us with questions if you want, too. I'll even tell you what firearms I'd consider most valuable (since there is no "one" firearm that does it all). As I said, I have not been a serious big game hunter, but I've done some (probably more than most people excepting the serious guys who haven't missed an opening day, for any game or fowl, for 40 years). I'm not a gunsmith, or a special forces operative, but I've been in law enforcement for 35 years and I do know handguns, some rifles, lots of shotguns, calibers and gauges, etc. and I do have my opinion on what's good to have (especially if you can only have a few), and which are good self-defense weapons and which are not, and what are good hunting guns and what are not.

I have been asked, and while I'm a bit reluctant to do so, I'll add here that if I could have <u>only one</u> firearm, it would be the Ruger 10/22. It is a quality rifle, it is inexpensive, its ammunition is inexpensive, it's dependable, and it's accurate. With the right round (the Remington .22 Caliber, 33 grain, hollow point, "Yellow Jacket", at 1500 feet per second), it is a hard-hitting, lethal combination for everything except big game. Another good choice of .22 ammo is the Velocitor 40 grain hollow point. If you question my assertion that .22 caliber long rifle is lethal, go here: http://www.youtube.com/watch?v=xAkOzr6 cDx0 Of course, good bullet placement on your target is always the primary objective. And, when TSHTF (as James Wesley Rawles, author of the best seller, How To Survive The End Of The World As We Know It, said), "Keep common ammunition for barter"; .22 caliber long rifle ammunition is common and will be more available than any other, and most accepted as barter. .223 caliber, .45 caliber, and 12 gauge shotgun rounds will be valuable as well.

I wasn't going to make any statement beyond the "one gun", but while allowing a few fellow preppers to read the proof of Survive Doom, they asked what else would I have, if say... only four guns. So without going into the specifics as to why, here they are: the Ruger 10/22 using the ammunition mentioned above. The Glock 21 .45 caliber pistol, using Black Hills .45 230 grain hollow points. The Remington Model 870 12 gauge CMB pump shotgun with 23"/28" dual combination barrels and synthetic stock, using 3" Mag. Remington, 00 Buck for self defense, 2 1/2" or 3" No. 7 Shot for fowl hunting, 2 3/4" Sabot Slug for large game. And finally, an AR 15 .223 caliber, scoped using Remington .223 UMC 55 grain, full metal jacket ammo.

For the technical questions and perhaps more sophisticated information about guns and ammo, you can always go to guys like Chuck Hawkes, John Leinbaugh, Randy Garret, or myriad other gun gurus or gun forums. If your questions or concerns are not about guns, but anything else the "survivalist" must know, I can say there are literally hundreds of informative books available and of course, the Internet is loaded with all kinds of information and survival blogs, along with www.survivedoom.com. Use your resources while you can. After all, this book isn't to provide you with everything you must have or know, but to spur you into action; TO GET YOU TO WRAP YOUR HEAD AROUND GETTING PREPARED. Time may be running short.

We have had the fortunate opportunity to consult with some rather serious and wealthy survival preppers, helping them to maximize their preparedness. Our consultation services are available, with very reasonable hourly or (complete or partial) project rates. We have the resources already in place to help you with your homework in getting prepared. Just contact us through the website, (http://www.survivedoom.com).

Product Samplings

Regarding the B.O.B., below is a "tasting" (very limited suggestion list) of products we've researched, bought, like and recommend. It's by no means an extensive or comprehensive list, just some ideas. You can see we shop all over the place. For example, you don't need to spend $5.00 on a fancy lighter; a 3 pack of Bic lighters is available at the 99 cent store. We use our imagination and improvise. You should too.

10" Folding Pruning Saw, Amazon: **$15.49**
http://amzn.to/HSHFyh

Folding Shovel, Rothco, Amazon: **$11.47**
http://amzn.to/Jj3DpA

Nylon String, 225' roll, Amazon: **$5.76**
http://amzn.to/IXlWVA

Combat Knife: M Tech, Full Tang, Stainless Steel Jungle Survival Knife **$17.79**
http://amzn.to/IBquO1

Magnifying Glass 2" 10x, Amazon: **$3.63**
http://amzn.to/IBqIEJ

Water Canteen, GI Issue, 1 quart, $4.60 x 3 = **$13.80**
http://amzn.to/IXnpv0

Headlamp, Cree 300 Lumen Hiking Headlamp, Amazon: **$14.80**
http://amzn.to/HVBF5b

Emergency Radio, Sony ICF S-10K2 Pocket AM-FM Mini AA Battery **$16.25**
http://amzn.to/JgusPT
I have this radio and it's awesome. I've run it for 3 years and never had to put in new batteries. It gets better reception than my desktop radio. I don't think a weather radio is all that necessary because any station broadcasting will give weather information.

Parachute Chord, 50' hank **$4.40**
http://amzn.to/I1I3H3.

Matches, ECO Green Strike Anywhere, Blue Diamond Brand, 300 Count Box. **$5.85**
http://amzn.to/JayTIm

5-in-1 Survival Whistle, Match Case **$3.70**
http://amzn.to/I9D0pE

Storm Proof Matches, Orange Tube, 30
Count, **$6.99**
http://amzn.to/HVCLOe

Bic Style Lighter
3 for **$1.00** @ 99 Cent Store

Fire Starter Pellets, 1 lb. jar, **$9.54**
http://amzn.to/I5t9lo
Package in a 2oz container, 12pk: **$12.95**
http://amzn.to/HWjQo9

Swedish Magnesium Steel / Flint Strike
Match   **$4.53**
http://amzn.to/HWJxWA

Mineral Spirits 1gal, Home Depot **$14.97**
2 oz. Plastic Bottle, 12pk: **$10.95**
http://amzn.to/I5tUe1

Binoculars
Tasco Essentials 10x25mm, Camo, **$14.17**
http://amzn.to/I5ufNT

One Hand Folding Knife, Gerber STL 2.0,
Fine Edge **$9.64**
http://amzn.to/I1QS45

Leatherman Wingman Multi-Tool **$26.95**
http://amzn.to/HWKvlu

Duct Tape 1 7/8" x 160', Silver **$6.22**
http://amzn.to/I7Mv56

Flashlight, LED 220 Lumen, Nebo Redline,
3 AAA Batteries, **$24.17**
http://amzn.to/HWLbrh

Leather Gloves, Wells Lamont #1132-L
Large Grain Leather, **$14.91**
http://amzn.to/HWLm5V
I don't believe the BOB needs 2 pairs of
gloves. 1 High Quality pair of leather
gloves, I believe, will suffice. At least they
have in my off roading experience.

Rain Poncho **$15.00**.

Compass, SE Military Lensatic with pouch.
$9.50
http://amzn.to/HLg1iP
this compass is more than adequate for a 72
hour BOB.

Dishwasher soap, 12 ozs. $1.00

Fill 4 oz. bottles, 6pk, **$6.59**
http://amzn.to/HSRgoP

Hand Sanitizer & Handi-wipes small pkgs.
$1.00 ea.

Camera, Cannon PowerShot A1300, uses AA
Batteries, **$119.00**
http://amzn.to/HTZp7H

Shop Towels, 25 pk, Amazon: **$9.54**
http://amzn.to/HU021a

First Aid Kit, Coleman Weekender, **$16.99**
http://amzn.to/HU0lsN

Fence Tool Pliers, Michigan Industrial Tool.
or Olympia Tool **$10.99**
http://amzn.to/JjrqFQ

Tarp, 8'X10', Camo, TexSport, **$12.56**
http://amzn.to/JaPStS

Sun Block, Lip and Face Screen, Beyond
Coastal Brand, **$5.85**
http://amzn.to/JjtBJH

Insect Repellent: 100% Deet Spray, 1 oz
Bottle, **$9.53**
http://amzn.to/HVHO1d

Batteries, Spare, 6 AAA, (3 - LED
Flashlight, and 3 - LED Headlamp), 4
AA (Emergency Radio)

Mirror, Stainless, Coghlins, **$5.94**
http://amzn.to/HWP6UV

Road Flare, 30 Minute Fusee, $2.73 ea. x 2
= **$5.46**
http://amzn.to/HVIbIV

Reflector Tape, Red, JVCC REF 7, 1" X
30', **$12.81**
http://amzn.to/HSU3OM

Can Opener, P51, Rothco, 10 pack, $5.20
= **$1.02 ea.**
http://amzn.to/Jjvg1K

Wax Candle, White, 3/4" X 6" 3 for **$1.00**
99 Cents Store

Mini Emergency Travel Sewing Kit, **$1.97**
http://amzn.to/JaTgFe

Floss, **$1.00**
99 Cent Store

Mylar Emergency Space Blanket, 10pk @
$7.99
http://amzn.to/HLmRVM

Neosporin Antibacterial Ointment, 99 Cent
Store
0.5 Oz. size, **$1.00**

Hydrogen Peroxide, CVS or Walmart, 16 Oz
Bottle, $1.97
2 oz. Plastic Bottle, 12pk: **$10.95**
http://amzn.to/I5tUe1

Cup, Aluminum Canteen Style, Rothco,
$5.78
http://amzn.to/HW5ypb

Water Purification; household bleach, $1.40
Gal.
2 oz. Plastic Bottle, 12pk: **$10.95**
http://amzn.to/I5tUe1
**3 drops per quart purifies water for
drinking**. 12 drops (1/4 teaspoon) purifies 1
gallon.

Plastic Containers: www.usplastic.com

OF COURSE, we'd like to build the B.O.B. for you. You can choose from a variety of products, using our system concept. Whether it's BOB ONE (for 7 days), or BOB ONE and BOB TWO (for 30 days or more), or the great little BOB BOTTLE (a compact little kit of survival items that can be kept in your car's glove box).

OUR BOB SYSTEM WILL SAVE YOU TIME AND IT WILL SAVE YOU MONEY. IT WILL ARRIVE READY TO GRAB AND GO. WE'VE DONE THE THINKING, TRIALS AND TESTING, PURCHASING, AND PACKING FOR YOU. YOU CAN HAVE CONFIDENCE IN IT, AND YOU CAN COUNT ON IT WHEN YOU NEED IT.

AVAILABLE AT:
WWW.SURVIVEDOOM.COM

NOTE: If we build a B.O.B. for you, we reserve the right to substitute different brands and items (without sacrificing confidence.)

Notes (where you get to include items you've found):

_____

_____

_____

_____

_____

_____

_____

_____

_____

_____

_____

_____

_____

_____

_____

_____

_____

_____

_____

_____

_____

_____

_____

INDEX